SHRUBS AND VINES FOR ATLANTIC CANADA

Choose the best plants for your location

Also published by Boulder Books

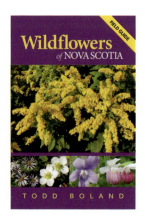
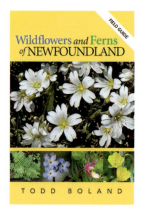
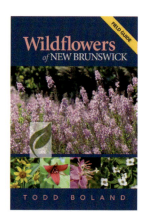
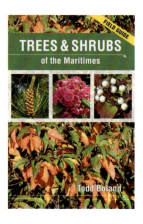
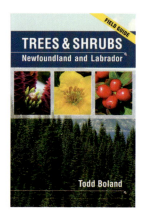
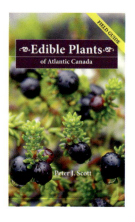
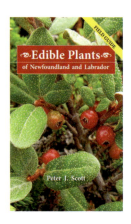
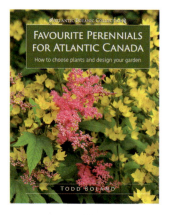

SHRUBS AND VINES FOR ATLANTIC CANADA

Choose the best plants for your location

TODD BOLAND

Library and Archives Canada Cataloguing in Publication

Title: Shrubs and vines for Atlantic Canada : choose the best plants for your location / Todd Boland.
Names: Boland, Todd, author.
Description: "Atlantic botanic collection". | Includes bibliographical references and index.
Identifiers: Canadiana 20210148144 | ISBN 9781989417287 (softcover)
Subjects: LCSH: Shrubs—Atlantic Provinces—Handbooks, manuals, etc. | LCSH: Climbing plants—Atlantic Provinces—Handbooks, manuals, etc. | LCGFT: Handbooks and manuals.
Classification: LCC SB435.6.C32 A85 2021 | DDC 582.17/09715—dc23w

© 2021 Todd Boland

Published by Boulder Books
Portugal Cove-St. Philip's, Newfoundland and Labrador
www.boulderbooks.ca

Design and layout: Todd Manning
Editor: Stephanie Porter
Copy editor: Iona Bulgin

All photos by Todd Boland

Printed in Canada

Excerpts from this publication may be reproduced under licence from Access Copyright, or with the express written permission of Boulder Books Ltd., or as permitted by law. All rights are otherwise reserved and no part of this publications may be reproduced, stored in a retrieval system, or transmitted in any form or by any means, electronic, mechanical, photocopying, scanning, recording, or otherwise, except as specifically authorized.

We acknowledge the financial support of the Government of Newfoundland and Labrador through the Department of Tourism, Culture, Industry and Innovation.

CONTENTS

Introduction 7

    Using shrubs and vines in a garden 13

    Some aspects of soil 18

    Garden maintenance 22

    Special gardens 30

    Gardens of note in Atlantic Canada 34

    Shrubs and vines at a glance 35

Shrubs 41

Ericaceous Shrubs 133

Conifers 159

Vines 179

Plant selector 200

Index: Plants by Latin name 204

Index: Plants by common name 206

Acknowledgements 209

About the author 210

Introduction

In 2018 I wrote my first gardening book, *Favourite Perennials for Atlantic Canada*. This publication is a complement to that book, introducing Atlantic Canadian gardeners to my favourite shrubs and climbers. I have over 40 years of gardening experience in the Atlantic Canada region, specifically in St. John's, Newfoundland and Labrador, and I am well aware of the challenges our climate and geology present.

While some perennials may be difficult to grow in Atlantic Canada, shrubs and climbers may be more so, as they may not have the protection of an insulating blanket of snow in winter. My earliest experience with gardening as a teenager was primarily growing perennials, but I also cultivated a few shrubs and vines. The first vine I grew was common honeysuckle, *Lonicera periclymenum*. This highly fragrant vine has been grown by Atlantic Canadian gardeners for over 100 years and is considered a heritage plant. Mine came as a slip from my great-aunt: she passed a stem to me in the spring and instructed me to stick it in the ground. I was dubious, but it leafed and, presto, I had a new plant! My mock-orange, *Philadelphus coronarius* (another heritage plant), arrived in a similar fashion, and it too rooted from a branch stuck in the ground. Forty years later I still have these two plants in my garden.

As a career, I worked at a plant nursery, led botanical tours across Newfoundland teaching visitors to the diversity of native plants, and taught horticulture at a community college. Then I finally landed my dream job of working at the Memorial University of Newfoundland Botanical Garden. I consider myself very fortunate that my passion is also my career.

My second hobby, photography, has gone hand in hand with gardening. I have amassed a huge photographic library—every plant I see, native or ornamental, is a subject. Photography lets me

SHRUBS AND VINES FOR ATLANTIC CANADA

see familiar flowers in a new light. I like to share my photos, and social media offers many ways to do that. Through gardening websites like Dave's Garden, garden forums, Flickr, Facebook, and Instagram, my photos have made the rounds. Little did I know that this would result in being invited to give talks to gardening groups across North America, the United Kingdom, and even as far away as New Zealand. During these trips I have met talented gardeners, several of whom became my mentors.

Ultimately, my love of plants and photography culminated in my being asked to write a series of field guides to the trees, shrubs, and wildflowers of Atlantic Canada for Boulder Books. With that task completed, I was ready to move on to a new project—a series of books devoted to Atlantic Canadian gardeners. With my favourite perennials book complete, it was time to describe my favourite shrubs and vines.

Doing the Latin dance

Have you ever noticed how different geographical regions have different names for the same plant? For example, the common names serviceberry, juneberry, Saskatoon berry, and shadblow all refer to the same shrub, *Amelanchier*. Common hazel and witch-hazel might appear to be related on the basis of their common name, but they are not. Partridgeberry in Nova Scotia refers to the plant *Mitchella repens*; in Newfoundland, that common name refers to an unrelated plant, *Vaccinium vitis-idaea* (a blueberry relative), which also goes by the common names lingonberry, rock cranberry, or mountain cranberry. Are you confused yet?

Vaccinium vitis-idaea.

Hydrangea macrophylla Cityline® Rio aka 'Ragra'.

Botanists have long known that assigning common names to plants introduces problems when they have to communicate with those from other regions, especially in different languages. Even gardeners from the same region have different common names for the same plant. That's why you'll often encounter scientific names when you look up information on a particular plant. As a student of botany, I embrace these scientific names, but I know they make many gardeners' eyes glaze over. However, as a rule, most botanical literature uses scientific names. The names are not difficult to understand once you get used to them, and you probably know more scientific names than you think—*Weigela*, *Viburnum*, and *Hydrangea* are scientific names that are also used as common names.

Scientific names for all living organisms follow a binomial nomenclature or two-name system. All names are written in Latin (the scientific name is informally called a Latin name). Latin was traditionally the language of scholars but is now considered a dead language (no nationality *speaks* Latin). The use of Latin to name plants—and all other species—is now a worldwide convention.

The first part of the scientific name identifies the genus to which the organism belongs. Different plants belonging to the same genus are closely related to each other. The second part identifies a specific group of genetically similar individuals: the species within the genus. The first letter of the genus name is always capitalized, while that of the species is in lowercase. Both words are italicized. For example, the genus *Syringa* is the scientific name used for most lilacs worldwide. As a gardener, you may know of many types of lilac—common lilac, dwarf lilac, Hungarian lilac, and Preston lilac, to name a few. To distinguish the specific types, each is given its own species name. The common lilac is called *Syringa vulgaris*; the Hungarian lilac, *Syringa josikaea*. The genus name *Syringa* denotes that they are related to each other, but the species name identifies each type of lilac. Scientific names, although difficult to pronounce, spell, and remember, make communication about living organisms more organized.

For all of these reasons, the shrubs and vines described in this book are listed alphabetically by scientific name. Think of it as an introductory lesson in botany.

•••

You'll also find terms like subspecies and cultivar in this book. Some wild plants naturally have a wide distributional range. Throughout their range, certain plant populations may be geographically isolated from others of their species by mountain ranges or oceans. These isolated plants are usually slightly different, genetically and physically, from the main population. If unique populations exist from the main population, they are often referred to as a subspecies, often abbreviated by "ssp." Subspecies names are always italicized. For example, black elderberry, *Sambucus nigra*, ranges across much of Europe, as well as eastern North America and along the Rocky Mountains. The European population is *Sambucus nigra* ssp. *nigra*. Populations in eastern North America differ genetically and physically and are named *Sambusuc nigra* ssp. *canadensis*. Those in the Rockies have blue fruit rather than black: *Sambucus nigra* ssp. *caerulea*.

A cultivar means "cultivated variety." Cultivars are selected and cultivated by humans. Some cultivars originate as mutations on plants, while others could be hybrids (crosses of two different plant species). "Named cultivars" are clones, which means that all plants with that name are genetically identical to each other. Propagating a cultivar must be done vegetatively through cuttings, grafting, or tissue culture—if it was grown from seed, the offspring of a named cultivar may look quite different from the parent. A cultivar name is always enclosed in single quotation marks and never italicized. Older cultivar names are often Latin names. For example, the silverleaf dogwood is *Cornus sericea* 'Elegantissima'. More modern cultivar names are written in English, such as *Cornus sericea* 'Prairie Fire'.

The term "selection" is often interchangeable with "cultivar" (but not always: a selection may occur in a wild plant or by human manipulation/hybridizing; a cultivar is always created by humans). You may also encounter "cultivar series," a group of named cultivars which appear similar in height and habit but may differ in flower or leaf colour. An example is the Cityline® Series of hydrangea. These are all the same height and growth habit but come in a variety of flower colours, each of which has a named cultivar: Cityline® Mars (bicoloured flowers), Cityline® Rio (lavender-blue), and Cityline® Paris (deep pink).

The symbol ® follows some series names; other times a series name is followed by the symbol ™. The symbol ® means that the plant name is a registered trademark name; ™ means it is an unregistered trademark name. Many ™ names become ® names in time. The use of trademarked names is a way for plant hybridizers and commercial producers of new plants to distinguish and brand their new plant releases. These trademarked names are usually the common name of the plant most often used in the nursery trade and, hence, the name most familiar to gardeners. Trademarked names are never enclosed in quotation marks. All trademarked plants have a proper cultivar name, which is placed within quotation marks, but we rarely see these names. For example, Cityline® Rio hydrangea has the proper name *Hydrangea macrophylla* 'Ragra', but in the nursery trade it is only labelled as Hydrangea Cityline® Rio.

WHAT IS A SHRUB?

The ornamental plants that we grow in our gardens fall into two broad groups—woody plants and herbaceous plants. Herbaceous plants generally dieback to the ground in winter and resprout from the base each spring. These plants are further divided into annuals, biennials, and perennials. Annuals, most often grown from seed each year, flower all summer and perish in winter, and are often referred to as bedding plants. Biennials germinate and produce a rosette of leaves in their first year, survive the winter, then send up flowering stems in their second summer; they generally die in their second winter. Perennials live for at least three years and more commonly grace our gardens for many years.

Woody plants do not dieback to the ground in winter; rather, their woody stems remain above ground year-round. This generally results in plants that become broader and/or taller with time. These include trees, shrubs, and vines; the latter two are the focus of this book.

Shrubs and vines make up the skeleton of the garden, providing structure, defining garden "rooms," and contributing to privacy or windbreaks. Some have flamboyant floral displays, like lilacs, weigela, and clematis. Others are grown primarily for their colourful leaves, such as ninebark, elderberry, and purple-leaved grape. Because their stems are present all winter, some shrubs, such as flame willow, red-osier dogwood, and broom, offer winter interest. Boxwood, holly, and Japanese andromeda are evergreen, so their foliage is appreciated year-round. Some shrubs and vines have spectacular fall foliage, such as burning bush and Boston ivy. Others, like cotoneaster and beautyberry, offer colourful fruit that persist into early winter. Others have interesting growth habits: rockspray cotoneaster, corkscrew hazel, or weeping hemlock. Shrubs and vines can offer much more to a garden than herbaceous plants alone and are indispensable additions to any landscape.

So what is a shrub? Most guides define a shrub as a woody plant having multiples stems and growing less than 6 metres tall. Trees generally have one or only a limited number of main stems and usually grow over 6 metres in

height. Arborists go one step further in defining a shrub as having stems less than 5 centimetres in diameter at a height of 140 centimetres above the ground, while trees have stems over 5 centimetres in diameter at that height. However, nature is never black and white, and there are exceptions. For example, serviceberry, *Amelanchier*, may have many stems and reach 3 to 4 metres tall—or may be trained into a tree with one main trunk and reach 8 metres. Technically, it can be a shrub or a tree. For the purpose of this book, any woody plants that has a shrublike form will be included.

Vines are woody plants whose stem requires support. It may be a plant supported by training it up trellises, pergolas, or arbours, such as climbing roses. Most vines have their own adaptations for support: tendrils such as Virginia creeper, specialized stem roots on English ivy, or a twining habit by wisteria.

Using shrubs and vines in a garden

Planning a garden, especially if gardening is new to you, can be a daunting task. As shrubs form the skeleton of a garden, they need to be positioned before you decide on bedding plants and perennials.

To start, make a sketch of what you would like in your garden. When purchasing a plant, always look at its label: not only does it provide the plant's scientific name but also its light requirements, hardiness, and overall size. Water requirements, blooming season, and other characteristics may also be included. Such information is essential in planning your garden. Ideally, a garden should be attractive all seasons; shrubs and vines are the essential component to provide this.

Several points need to be considered when you select shrubs and vines for your garden.

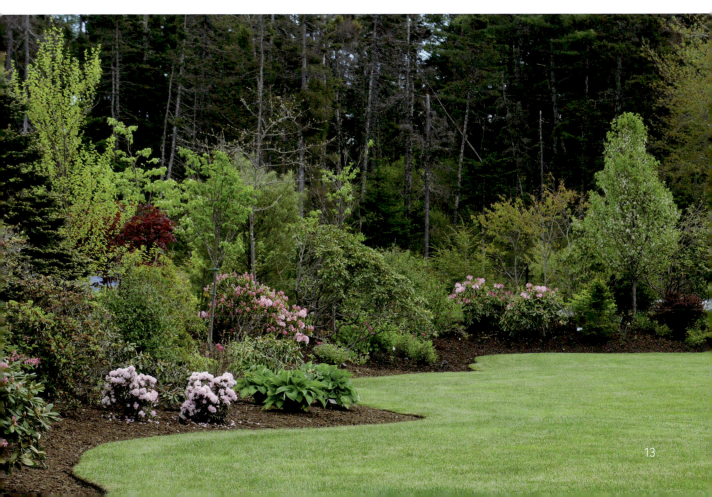

1. Hardiness

Agriculture Canada's hardiness rating system is based primarily on the minimum winter temperature. The US Department of Agriculture (USDA) has a similar system, although it is not as detailed as the Canadian system. In both systems, the ratings range from 0 to 10: 0, the High Arctic; 10, essentially tropical. The USDA system ratings are whole numbers: zones 4, 5, or 6. In Canada, the zones are subdivided into "a" or "b." For example, you may be in zone 4a or zone 4b: "a," the colder end of zone 4; "b," the milder end.

As noted earlier, plant tags usually indicate the hardiness zone. Once you know what zone you are in, you can select the proper plants. If you wish to err on the side of caution, select a plant that is rated a zone lower than your growing zone (e.g., a zone 4 plant if you live in zone 5). On the other hand, some gardens have milder

Atlantic Canada plant hardiness zones

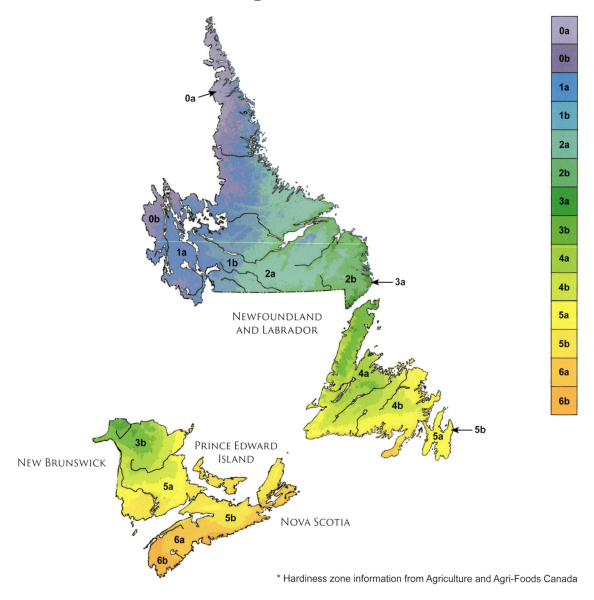

* Hardiness zone information from Agriculture and Agri-Foods Canada

14

A foundation planting featuring dwarf Alberta spruce and weeping French pussywillow.

microclimates and you might be successful in growing a plant that is not rated hardy for your area, such as a zone 6 plant in zone 5. As you become more familiar with both plants and your zone, you may want to experiment to see what will survive in your area.

Keep in mind that herbaceous perennials, since they dieback to the ground each winter, allow for more experimentation with hardiness than shrubs and vines. Because shrubs and vines are taller, with stems often held above the snow level, they are exposed to more extreme weather. Thanks to climate change, gardeners in Atlantic Canada are experiencing windier winter conditions and more extreme temperature fluctuations than even two decades ago. Broad-leaved shrubs are particularly susceptible to winter conditions and need to be properly positioned for success.

2. PLANTING LOCATION

Where will the shrub be located? In front of a fence? Free-standing as a specimen in the middle of a lawn? Grown as a foundation plant along the side of a house or a driveway? Underplanted beneath taller trees? Positioned close to the sea or a busy highway? Will the vine grow up the front of a house, trained along a pergola or arbour, or allowed to scramble through a tree?

If your planting area is exposed to brutal northwest winter winds, broad-leaved evergreens may not work. Even a gardener in zone 5 may lose a zone 4 holly if it is exposed to cold winter winds. The same may apply to coniferous evergreens. Dwarf Alberta spruce is rated hardy to zone 3 but if you plant it on an exposed hill in zone 5, it may perish or exhibit winter burn on the windward side. Exposure to roadside or coastal

salt spray will also limit many shrubs and vines. Broad-leaved evergreens and conifers are often more susceptible to salt than deciduous shrubs. As a rule, deciduous shrubs and vines are more reliable in potentially problematic locations such as those listed above. On the other hand, your planting area may be within a sheltered courtyard. This may provide a warmer microclimate, allowing you to grow a zone 5 plant in a zone 4 area.

3. LIGHT

Light can make or break a good garden display. Too often, new gardeners purchase a plant impulsively without realizing its light requirements. Usually, it is a sun-lover that ends up being planted in too much shade. Over time, the plant's health deteriorates or it becomes leafy with few flowers. As a rule, most plants grown for their impressive floral displays are sun-lovers, while those grown primarily for their attractive foliage will tolerate more shade. There are, however, exceptions on both sides.

Observe your potential planting area from sunrise to sunset to determine how much light the area receives. Is it sunny all day or does it only get morning, midday, or late afternoon sun? If the area is most often shady, is the shade dense (like under evergreen trees or along the north side of a house or solid fence) or is it dappled (such as under small-leaved deciduous trees)? A white neighbouring house or building may reflect light onto the north side of your house, providing bright shade. Shrubs planted under deciduous trees often receive nearly full sun in spring but dense shade in summer.

Shrubs growing in dappled shade.

4. SOIL MOISTURE

What is the moisture level in the soil of the planting area? Under trees, the soil is likely to be dry, as the overhead canopy acts as an umbrella and the trees absorb any soil moisture faster than the underplanted shrubs. Sunny slopes are also apt to be dry, as are gravelly or sandy soils. In these locations, select drought-tolerant plants. If irrigation is not a problem, this is not critical, but as many municipalities practice water conservation, it is better to work with nature and grow drought-resistant plants in dry areas.

Low-lying areas, on the other hand, may be moist, if not downright soggy, especially in spring as the snow melts. It can be more challenging to overcome this wetness than drought, and it is better to select plants that can tolerate such conditions. Shrubs and vines at a glance, starting on page 35, provides a reference list of plants for the driest and wettest sites.

5. PLANT SIZE AND LAYOUT

Once you have determined the characteristics of the growing area, you are ready to select the plants. Another common mistake made by new gardeners is not realizing how large a plant will become. When you purchase a shrub, it is often a young plant only two or three years old, showing no potential of its ultimate size. It is hard to imagine a 60-centimetre-tall mock-orange shrub eventually reaching 5 metres tall. Shrubs are too often overplanted or become too large for their allotted space. While this may not be problematic for the first few years, with time the shrubs may become overgrown, destroying the aesthetics of the original planting. Always refer to the plant's tag or to this book for overall dimensions.

It is also important that the shrub be in scale with the planting area. Within a courtyard, it is better to use smaller, narrow shrubs rather than tall, broad-spreading types. If growing shrubs along a foundation, make sure your selection remains low enough to prevent blocking adjacent windows. Along driveways, lower shrubs are better than tall ones.

6. THINK ALL-SEASON INTEREST

The wonderful thing about shrubs and vines is that, with the proper selection, you can provide year-round interest in any landscape. The blooming season of shrubs starts with spring heath, witch-hazel, and February daphne, all of which bloom by April. The last of the flowering shrubs are rose-of-Sharon and heathers, which bloom into October. Cotoneaster and holly have attractive berries which can last all winter. Some shrubs are grown primarily for their colourful leaves, which may be variegated white or yellow or pure yellow or purple. Others produce fall colours in vibrant shades of yellow, orange, red, or purple. Broad-leaved evergreens and dwarf conifers can look as good in winter as they do in summer. Some deciduous shrubs have spectacularly coloured stems that brighten up a snowy landscape. There is no reason not to have a spectacular year-round garden if you select the right complement of shrubs and vines.

Some aspects of soil

WHAT IS SOIL?

Soil, the upper layer of earth, usually contains both inorganic and organic components. It anchors plants and provides water and nutrients. The inorganic or mineral component includes both the soil particles and, as many gardeners in Atlantic Canada realize, plenty of rocks. The larger soil particles are sand. Sandy soils are generally well drained but poor at retaining nutrients and prone to dryness. Clay particles are the smallest and result in dense, poorly drained,

18   SHRUBS AND VINES FOR ATLANTIC CANADA

but often nutrient-rich, soil. Silt particles are between the size of sand and clay, and silty soils have the best qualities of sandy and clay soils.

How can you tell if your soil is sandy or clay? Roll some moist (but not soggy) soil between your fingers. If the texture is like sandpaper, it is sandy soil; if the soil rolls like putty, it is clay; if it has a silky feel, silt dominates. Gardening books often cite loam as the ultimate soil type. Loam is simply soil that contains nearly equal amounts of sand, silt, and clay and thus is reasonably fertile and well drained but holds some moisture.

Soil also has an organic component: plant particles and living organisms such as worms, beetles, fungus, and bacteria. All are essential to healthy soil. Gardeners can alter the organic plant-based component by adding organic material. Peat is perhaps the most popular soil amendment, but various composts, store-bought or home-made, are also ideal. Compost may add needed nutrients, but peat does not. However, both improve the quality of mineral soil (heavy in silt, sand, and/or clay). When added to a sandy soil, organic material adds nutrients and helps with moisture retention; added to a clay soil, it loosens the soil structure and improves drainage.

SOIL DEPTH
One of the most critical factors to creating a successful perennial bed is the depth of the soil. Ideally, the planting location for most shrubs should have a minimum of 60 centimetres of properly prepared soil. This can be challenging if you live in a typical city lot where the topsoil has been scraped away prior to house construction, with just 15 centimetres of often poor-quality soil brought back for laying the prescribed landscape sods before the house is sold. Shallow, poor-quality soil results in weak plants that are prone to drying out. Properly prepared soil of the proper

depth is key to a healthy shrub bed. If the planting area is simply too rocky to create a soil bed that is 60 centimetres deep, use raised beds filled with soil.

SOIL PH
Gardening books often state that "this plant prefers acidic soil" or "this plant prefers alkaline soil." Sometimes specific pH ranges are given; for example, rhododendrons prefer a soil pH of 4.5 to 6. Soil pH is the measure of its acidity or alkalinity. The pH ranges from 0 to 14: 0, very acidic; 14, very alkaline; 7, neutral. Lemon juice, which is acidic, has a pH of about 2. Bleach is alkaline, with a pH of 12.6. Soil usually ranges from pH 3.5 to 9. Generally, areas with high rainfall have acidic soil, while dry regions have alkaline soil. In Atlantic Canada, which is relatively wet, most soils range from 4.5 to 6, which is on the acidic side; consequently, it is ideal for rhododendrons, heaths, and heathers. As a rule, most plants prefer soil with a pH of 5.5 to 7.5.

If a plant prefers acidic soil but is exposed to a higher pH, it will likely have difficulty absorbing iron, a needed micronutrient. The leaves become chlorotic, turning yellow but often retaining green veins. On the other hand, if a plant prefers neutral to alkaline soil and is exposed to acidic soil, aluminium toxicity can kill the active root tips, leading to stunted growth with cupped or wrinkled leaves.

Ideally, measure your soil pH with a pH kit. If your soil is 5.5 or higher, you should be able to grow almost all of the shrubs and vines described in this book. If it is below 5.5, a copious dusting of lime each year raises the pH to suitable levels. Alternatively, select shrubs which can tolerate acidic soil, such as rhododendrons and their relatives. Refer to the special gardens section on acidic gardens, page 31, for more details on this group of shrubs. Shrubs listed as prefer-

Rhododendrons require acidic soil.

ring neutral to alkaline soil should be annually dusted with lime, unless your soil is above pH 7.

Planting shrubs and vines

Once you have assessed the environment of the planting area and prepared the soil properly, it is time to plant. Shrubs and vines are either sold as bareroot, bagged, or container-grown. In the case of shrubs and vines, generally only hedging material is sold as completely bareroot plants. Such plants must be put in the ground when the plant is dormant, before leafing in spring or after leaf-drop in fall. It is imperative that the roots not dry out during the planting process, so keep them in water or wrapped in damp burlap until planting. The planting hole should be large enough to accommodate the evenly spread roots of the plant; roots should never be bent or forced together into too small a planting hole. It is often useful to create a slight dome in the middle of the planting hole, then position the plant in the middle of the dome so that the roots are evenly spaced and angling downward. The newly planted shrub or vine should be planted at the same depth as it was in the nursery, which is indicated by a change in bark colour. Backfill soil around the roots and compact the soil to prevent air pockets. Water well, and if conditions are dry, water regularly for the first few weeks.

TODD BOLAND

Some shrubs and vines are offered early in the season, especially in box stores, as bagged or boxed plants. Clematis, Virginia creeper, and roses are often sold this way. They are often less expensive than container-grown plants. Keep in mind that these bagged or boxed plants are often sold too early for direct planting outdoors. If you wait until it is safe to plant them directly outside, they often become leggy or spindly. When this happens, they rarely develop into satisfactory plants. It is better to pot them and grow them indoors in a sunny, cool window until the risk of frost has passed; then plant them outside, treating them as a container-grown plant. For roses, if the weather permits, you can directly plant the "bagged" plant outdoors, following the same directions as for a bareroot plant, but position the graft union at or just above the soil surface to reduce the incidence of suckers arising from the rootstock.

Container-grown plants may be moved at any time during the growing season; however, in my experience, early in the season is best so that plants have a chance to send out new roots into the planting area before the ground freezes. The general rule of thumb for planting a container-grown plant is to make the planting hole twice as wide and 15 centimetres deeper than the container the plant is growing in. A standard nursery 2-gallon pot is approximately 22 centimetres wide and 22 centimetres tall, so the planting hole should be 44 centimetres wide and 37 centimetres deep. Dig the hole, placing 15 centimetres of good-quality soil in the hole. Take the plant out of its container; it should slide out with its roots intact. Gently loosen the root ball with your fingers. If the plant is root-bound, use a knife to make three or four 2- to 3-centimetre-deep slices longitudinally through the roots. The cut roots will then be stimulated to send out new ones. This is especially needed

for root-bound rhododendrons. Again, backfill and compact the soil, making sure that the plant is at the same depth as it was in its pot. Water well and water regularly if the weather is dry.

At some point you may have to move a shrub or vine from one part of your garden to another. The larger the plant, the more challenging this will be, as the root system may be quite large. The key to success is to move the plant with as much soil attached to the roots as possible. Like bareroot planting, the window of opportunity for transplanting a shrub or vine is limited to the dormant season—either before the plant has leaved or just after leaf-drop. Midsummer transplanting is rarely successful unless the plant has very fine, dense roots, such as ericaceous plants.

Garden maintenance

WATERING

Generally, well-established shrubs and vines do not require additional watering. Their roots are much deeper than those of annuals and perennials. However, newly planted shrubs and vines require thorough watering to help them become established. Because of global climate change, dry spells are becoming more frequent. All too often I see new gardeners splashing their plants with water, thinking that that will satisfy their moisture needs. Such light watering encourages shallow roots, which make plants even more prone to drought, and fungal diseases, slugs, and snails, all which thrive on wet foliage.

The rule of thumb: 1 inch of water once a week. It is best to give the garden a thorough soaking once a week. If using a sprinkler, place a pie pan in the middle of the watered area until 1 inch of water has gathered in it. It is also best to water in the morning so that the foliage will be dry by nightfall. This will reduce the incidence of fungal diseases and slug and snail activity.

Shrubs growing under trees will require more water, as trees outcompete shrubs for water and their canopy acts as an umbrella. Foundation plantings under eaves can also be prone to drought. Slopes, too, often become droughty, especially if south-facing. Sandy soil will dry more quickly than loamy or organically rich soil. If you have a spot that is prone to dryness and you do not want to be constantly watering, select drought-resistant plants. Shrubs and vines at a glance (page 35) provides choices.

Deadheading

Unless you plan to collect seeds from your shrubs and vines, it is best to deadhead as soon as the flowers fade. Deadheading prevents seed set. Essentially, plants produce flowers to set seed, their main form of reproduction, but this can be a strain on a plant. If a plant successfully sets seed, it may produce fewer flowers the following year. This is a way for them to save energy. This is especially true for plants that produce large trusses of flowers, like lilacs and rhododendrons. Left to their own devices, such shrubs only bloom well every second year. By deadheading, you can stimulate more regular flowering every year. Deadheading also makes plants look tidier and can reduce the incidence of disease. Rotting petals encourage fungal diseases to attack a plant.

Fertilizing

Some people never fertilize their gardens; others do so regularly. If your soil is healthy and you dig plenty of compost into it, you may not need additional fertilizer. This is especially true if you mulch the soil each year with leaf mould and compost.

If you suspect that your soil is not ideal and your shrubs or vines are not robust enough, the

Deadhead lilacs as soon as the flowers fade.

addition of chemical fertilizer is warranted. Water-soluble fertilizers are quicker acting but do not last as long as granular fertilizer. As a result, you may need to use water-soluble fertilizer every few weeks throughout the growing season. Granular fertilizers, on the other hand, are slow-acting; therefore, one application in spring is often enough. Follow the manufacturer's recommended application rates for your fertilizer choice. Fertilizers are salts and, if used too heavily, can do more harm than good.

Water-soluble fertilizers are often applied by hose applicators so that, as you water, you are fertilizing at the same time. Wetting the leaves of plants with this dilute fertilizer will not harm them. Granular fertilizers, however, are much more concentrated—never let it touch the plant's leaves or stems. Instead, apply it around the base of the plant but not touching it, just as new spring growth begins to appear. Scratch the fertilizer into the soil to speed up the dissolving rate.

Fertilizers come in many formulations. Generally, a three-number code, such as 10-15-10, is marked on the package. Each number represents, in order, the percentage amount of nitrogen, phosphorus, and potassium, commonly written as N, P, and K, in the fertilizer. These three elements are the macronutrients required by plants in relatively high doses. Nitrogen (N) allows for more leaves and faster growth. Many lawn fertilizers are high in nitrogen to encourage rapid growth and lush green grass. For flowering shrubs and vines, avoid fertilizers high in nitrogen, as these encourage leaves over flowers. Phosphorus (P) promotes fruit, flower, and better root production; fertilizers highest in the middle number are best for flowering shrubs and vines. Potassium (K) improves a plant's overall health, helps combat diseases, and improves winter hardiness. Some fertilizers also have trace elements

or micronutrients, such as iron, magnesium, or copper.

"Balanced fertilizers" are simply any fertilizers that contains N, P, and K. It does not mean that the three numbers are the same: 10-52-10, 20-20-20, and 15-30-15 are all balanced fertilizers. Non-balanced fertilizers are missing one of the main macronutrients. For example, bone meal, 2-13-0, has N and P but no K. The high amount of phosphorus, good for root production, is why bone meal is often used on transplants.

MULCHING

Mulch is basically anything laid over the ground to cover it. It reduces weeds or makes pulling them easier and can reduce the amount of watering required in the garden, as the mulch traps soil moisture. If available, one of the best mulches is shredded, partially composted leaves. Compost from kitchen and garden waste is also suggested. Both of these mulches act as an organic fertilizer and is applied in a 3- to 5-centimetre-thick layer every May-June.

Other popular mulches include shredded tree bark or bark nuggets. The problem with these mulches is that, in time, the bark rots. The breakdown of bark by fungi and bacteria requires nitrogen in order to be effective. This nitrogen, taken from the underlying soil, results in nitrogen deficiency and possible stunting of the plant's growth.

To reduce weeds, some new gardeners plant their shrubs in slits cut into landscape fabric. This fabric is covered by bark mulch, which lasts much longer, since the mulch is not in direct contact with the soil. However, strong winds can more easily blow bark mulch off the fabric. Spring bulbs can be attractive when planted

RIGHT: Mulched shrub beds featuring commercial shredded tree bark.

among shrubs, but if landscape fabric is used, this is not an option. The use of landscape fabric has pros and cons.

Winter Protection

The greatest detriment to shrubs and vines in winter is exposure to cold winds and breakage under heavy snow loads. For the most part, deciduous shrubs and vines can withstand cold winds unless you are growing a borderline hardy variety. If snow removal dumps extra snow on deciduous shrubs, plant breakage may result. Tying stems together with soft twine or nylon stockings often keeps them from becoming splayed under the snow. Dwarf upright conifers can suffer from exposure to both cold winds and snow load. The former often cause browning on the windward side; the latter can crush the plants, destroying their upright form. Building a teepee or box covered in burlap, or purchasing pre-made shrub covers can help protect them. Broad-leaved evergreens are even more susceptible to both cold wind and snow load, as their evergreen foliage is exposed to the worst of winter.

They too may benefit if protected under a burlap-covered frame. Avoid west, northwest, and northern exposures for broad-leaved evergreens, as those directions have the coldest winds. As a final note, never use plastic to cover plants in winter as this can heat up like a mini-greenhouse—a condition you don't want in the middle of winter.

Pruning

Unless you have provided your shrub or vine with plenty of space, there will come a time when the plant outgrows its allotted space and will need to be reduced in size. The removal of problem branches is called pruning. Pruning is perhaps the most stressful process for a new gardener to perform, but avoiding it exacerbates the problem. There are complete books devoted to the proper pruning of woody plants, but it need not be a daunting task. Here are a few pointers to get you started.

Broken, rubbing, diseased, or dead stems should be promptly removed whenever you see the damaged material. Such stems are breeding

Prune forsythia immediately after flowering.

places for diseases and insects. Simply cut the affected branches back to where the stems are healthy.

The main reason for pruning is to reduce the size of a plant. However, you should avoid a simple rounding or even cutting of the outer branches. That would be like placing a bowl on your head and cutting the hair that extends beyond—hairdressers would cringe at the idea. Hair is cut in different lengths, and so too a shrub. Trim back some branches more than others. You want an overall rounded effect but without that evenly pruned hedge effect. While that effect can work on a boxwood or privet, it is not aesthetically pleasing on a shrubby cinquefoil or viburnum.

The general rule for pruning: if a plant blooms in the spring, prune immediately after flowering. These plants bloom on last year's wood and set their flower buds in the previous autumn. Examples include February daphne, forsythia, and rhododendrons. Avoid spring-pruning these plants as it will remove that year's spring floral display. If the plant blooms mid- to late summer, then spring is the best time to prune. While you may destroy the blooms for that season, late-season bloomers often flower on current-season wood; you may still get a few blooms if the plant is spring-pruned, as with shrubby cinquefoil, hydrangea, and butterfly bush.

Reversions are growths on a plant that differ from the majority of the plant. Most often, reversions are seen as green leaves on an otherwise variegated or colourful-leaved plant or plain leaves on an otherwise lacy-leaved type of shrub. When you see such reversions, completely remove them back to the decorative foliage or you risk the entire shrub becoming like its wild ancestor.

Suckers are growths that arise from the rootstock of a grafted plant. The only shrubs regularly grafted are hybrid roses. If suckers arise, they are generally easy to spot, as they grow much faster than the main rose and have seven to nine, rather than five, leaflets per leaf. Suckers should be removed immediately back to the main stem.

The most severe form of pruning is coppicing or cutting back. This is the removal of all stems back to within a few inches of the ground and is done only when a shrub or vine becomes too old, leggy, or unsightly. Cutting back, done in early spring before the plants leaf, can completely rejuvenate a plant—although it may take a few years before a flowering shrub or vine resumes flowering. Popular shrubs that can be coppiced include lilac, spirea, viburnum, and shrubby cinquefoil.

One consolation about pruning most deciduous shrubs and vines is that they will recoup in time, even if pruned improperly. Broad-leaved evergreen shrubs and vines also recoup in time. This is not the case with conifers: they will not regenerate new growth if cut back into old wood. The exception is yew, which can be coppiced if necessary.

Among vines, clematis and wisteria have specific pruning requirements in order to provide maximum floral display. In late summer, wisteria should have all long twining growths pruned back to just three leaves per stem. This seems severe but results in the best flowering. It also keeps this vigorous vine in check. Clematis fall into three pruning groups. Group 1 clematis flower in late spring or early summer on growth from the previous year. You can prune these vines im-

mediately after they finish blooming in spring, but, more than likely, they will not require any pruning except for the removal of dead stems and occasional reduction in size due to being overly vigorous. *Clematis alpina* and *C. macropetala* belong to this group. Group 2 clematis have their main blooms in early to midsummer but can also produce scattered blooms later in the season. Many of the popular saucer-type clematis belong in this group. The easiest approach to pruning these clematis is to either prune the plant back by half in alternate years or to severely prune the plants back to within 30 centimetres of the ground every three to four years. Group 3 clematis flower in late summer or early autumn, blooming on current-season wood, and may be pruned to within 30 centimetres of the ground each spring. Clematis in this group include the texensis and viticella hybrids, Virgin's-bower as well as late bloomers like 'Jackmanii', Ernest Markham', 'Comtesse de Bouchard', and 'Ville de Lyon'. Alternatively, you can avoid pruning any of the above groups if you are content with a tangled mass of living and dead stems.

PROPAGATING SHRUBS

At some point you may want to increase the numbers of your favourite shrub or vine or maybe a friend has a hard-to-find selection that you must have. Shrubs can be propagated from seed or cuttings or by grafting. Although the cheapest and easiest method is by seed, the problem with this method is that most shrubs and vines offered by the landscape industry are hybrids. Seeds collected from hybrids rarely develop into plants that look like the parent. You may be lucky enough to get a better plant than the parent, but usually the resulting offspring is inferior. However, if the shrub or vine in question is a true species, then growing from seed is a perfect way to propagate it. February daphne, alpine clematis, and winter hazel are often propagated by seed. It should be noted that many shrub and vine seeds need a cold period before they will germinate; this stratification period can take from 8 to 12 weeks. To accommodate this, it is often easiest to sow these seeds in pots in the fall and leave the pots outdoors for the winter; the seeds should then germinate in the spring. Some species, such as holly and viburnum, can take two years for the seeds to germinate.

Grafting is a popular way to propagate dwarf conifers and some roses, and for the creation of standard shrubs (shrubs grafted onto a single stem to create a lollipop-like ornamental plant). Grafting is a specialized form of propagation rarely attempted by the home gardener.

By far the most popular way to propagate shrubs and vines is by cuttings. These fall into three groups: softwood, semi-hardwood, and hardwood. If you take a dormant twig of a shrub and simply push it into the ground and it roots, this in a loose sense is a hardwood cutting. Willows are commonly propagated this way. Commercially, hardwood cuttings are taken in late fall after leaf-drop. Unbranched, current-season stems, 15 to 20 centimetres long and pencil-sized, are cut from the shrub. The upper portion of the cutting is cut on a slant just above a bud. The bottom portion is cut flat across, then dipped into hormone powder, a horticultural product used to stimulate root development. The cuttings are placed in a container filled with sand, with their top 5 centimetres sticking out. They are then stored in a cold, frost-free place until spring, when they are stuck in the ground or in individual pots, where they should root and leaf as the spring progresses. For the home gardener, the easiest way to do hardwood cuttings is to take the stems as described above but, rather than placing them in sand for the winter, simply plant them directly in the garden and hope for the best. If it is a species that roots easily from hardwood cuttings, then it should work. Shrubs and vines that often root by this method include red-osier dogwood, deutzia, forsythia, kerria, twining honeysuckle, mock-orange, ninebark, rugose rose, elderberry, willow, and weigela.

Softwood cuttings are taken when the current-season growth is still flexible, usually late June or early July. Houseplants such as geranium, coleus, and ivy are taken as softwood cuttings. Only a few shrubs and vines will root in water. It is more popular to take semi-hardwood cuttings from mid-July to -August. For both softwood and semi-hardwood cuttings, take the tips of current-season wood, about 10 to 20 centimetres long, and remove the lower one-third of leaves. For plants with opposite (paired) leaves, make a clean cut immediately below the node, where a set of leaves was located. This is called a nodal cutting. If the plant has alternate leaves, make the cut just above where a leaf was located. This is an internodal cutting. Dip the cut end in hormone powder and place it in a rooting media. A 50-50 mixture of peat and sand or 50-50

Rooted cuttings ready for potting.

commercial potting soil and perlite is best. The rooting media needs to be moisture retentive but well aerated. Put the pot of cuttings in a clear plastic bag and place it in a bright but not sunny window. The bag will act like a mini-greenhouse and keep the humidity high around the cuttings. They will root within four to six weeks. The majority of deciduous shrubs and vines will root this way.

Cuttings of broad-leaved evergreen shrubs and dwarf conifers, as well as heaths, heathers, and their relatives, are generally taken as semi-hardwood cuttings in autumn. Dwarf conifer cuttings can be taken as late as January. Overall, these are much slower to root than summer deciduous cuttings and essentially require the use of specialized propagation equipment.

A final method of propagation is layering. This method takes advantage of shrubs and vines with long flexible stems. In spring, select a long flexible unbranched stem that is long enough to be partly buried under soil, with its top 15 centimetres or more sticking out of the soil. Make a cut one-third of the way through the stem at the point where it is buried. You may need to pin the stem into the ground to keep it secure. After about a year, the cutting should be sufficiently rooted and may be cut away from the parent. Many vines, along with forsythia, flowering quince, spirea, deutzia, beautybush, lace shrub, juniper, Siberian cypress, and blue holly, are possible subjects for layering.

Special gardens

Coastal Gardens

The more pervasive "problematic" area for gardening in Atlantic Canada is near the sea. The ocean is a significant part of our region, and plenty of gardeners live in areas that are kissed by the sea (if gale-force winds from the ocean with accompanying salt spray can be considered kissed).

The first challenge of coastal gardening is the wind. Coastal areas experience stronger winds than inland. Winds generated by both high- and low-pressure weather systems can hit the shore at full force, while locations even a few kilometres inland can have that force diminished by forests, buildings, and other objects. Rain and snow, when combined with wind, can do even more damage. To combat wind, gardeners should plant wind-resistant plants or erect windbreaks in the form of walls or fencing.

The second issue is salt spray, which accompanies wind. Wind can whip up salt spray from the water's surface. The stronger the wind, the saltier the water that will be generated. When this salt-laden spray hits plants, it often evaporates, further concentrating the salt on the leaves. Gardens within 300 metres of the shore are the most affected. Salt wicks water from the plant, resulting in conditions similar to being too dry. If too much salt accumulates on the plants' leaves or in the soil, the plants dehydrate and wilt. Evergreen shrubs and vines often develop brown margins or become "burnt" on the side facing the ocean. To overcome this, select plants that are salt- and drought-tolerant. On the positive side, plants grown by the sea often show less incidence of insect pests or fungal diseases than the same plant grown inland.

In summer, coastal regions are cooler than inland regions. Even on a calm day, there is little reprieve from sea breezes. Because the ocean is colder than the land, cooler ocean air is sucked inland as the warmer air rises. This can significantly lower temperatures along the immediate shoreline during the summer. Atlantic Canada is the foggiest part of Canada. Coastal fog lowers temperatures, particularly in the summer.

On the plus side, the ocean moderates winter temperatures, resulting in milder temperatures along the coast than inland, often allowing you to grow plants that are not generally considered hardy in your zone.

Another potential coastal issue is sandy soil. Some inland areas have excessively sandy soil, but coastal areas seem to have more than their share. Soil that is too sandy, while very well drained, can be prone to drought. Sandy soil, which is often infertile, can result in stunted growth. The problems with sandy soil are easily overcome by adding organic matter in the form of compost and/or peat.

Refer to Shrubs and vines at a glance (page 35) for a list of the best shrubs and vines to use in Atlantic Canadian coastal gardens.

Acidic Gardens—Ericaceous shrubs

A particular family of plants performs best under acidic soil conditions—the Ericaceae, commonly called the Heath, Heather, or Rhododendron family. Together they are referred to as the ericaceous shrubs. This group of plants is ecologically important in Atlantic Canada, as many of our native shrubs are members, including blueberries, cranberries, bilberries, huckleberries, sheep laurel, bog laurel, bog rosemary, rhodora, and leatherleaf. Nova Scotia's provincial floral emblem, the mayflower, is a member of the Ericaceae. As noted earlier, many of the native soils in Atlantic Canada are naturally acidic, so it is not surprising that our native shrubs are specifically adapted to such soil.

The Ericaceae also contains many highly

Rhododendrons and azalea are among the best shrubs for acidic gardens.

ornamental shrubs. In addition to rhododendrons, heaths, and heathers, ericaceous shrubs include mountain laurel, Japanese andromeda, wintergreens, and fetterbush. For a complete list, refer to Shrubs and Vines at a Glance. As a rule, these shrubs have exacting soil conditions and are therefore often grown in their own dedicated planting areas. The soil pH should be 4.5 to 6. They need well-drained soil that retains even moisture; they will not tolerate drought. A mixture of peat and sand with plenty of compost is ideal. For optimal blooming, most ericaceous shrubs require full sun in Atlantic Canada. However, some—wintergreen, fetterbush, and mountain laurel—tolerate part shade. As ericaceous shrubs have fine, shallow root systems, they benefit from an annual mulching of leaf mold, pine needles, or finely shredded bark.

Remember that many ericaceous shrubs become broad with age, so give them plenty of space. The larger rhododendrons are generally combined with other large ericaceous shrubs such as mountain laurel and Japanese andromeda, while smaller heaths and heathers are combined with other small ericaceous shrubs such as dwarf rhododendrons, mountain heather, bell heather, smaller wintergreens, and bog rosemary.

Wildlife Garden

So much land is being cleared for development that opportunities for wildlife to find food and shelter is becoming more challenging. As gardeners, we can help by planting shrubs and vines that benefit wildlife, in particular birds and pollinating insects. The plight of honeybees is well known to most gardeners: all over the world, honeybee populations are diminishing, due to a combination of diseases and parasites. Newfoundland is the last place on earth where hon-

Painted lady butterfly on butterfly bush.

eybees are still fairly healthy. However, honeybees are just one of a multitude of pollinators: native bees, wasps, butterflies, moths, beetles, hoverflies, and hummingbirds were pollinators in Atlantic Canada before the introduction of honeybees. Without these pollinators, we would have no vegetables or fruit and many of our flowering plants would be extinct, as they could not produce seed.

By providing shrubs with berries and placing bird feeders in strategic spots, we encourage birds to stay around our gardens, where they can eat plenty of insect pests during the summer season. Creating a wildlife-friendly garden is not only beneficial to pollinators but also to our own well-being. The flitting movement of pollinators and birds allow us to experience nature in our own backyards.

Wildlife need a home and a source of water and food. Bird baths provide water. Berries provide food for birds; nectar or pollen, for pollinators. The tubular flowers of weigela and beautybush attract bees. They, along with butterflies, also visit viburnum and spirea. Trumpet-creeper and honeysuckle vines act as hummingbird feeders.

As for wildlife homes, you can provide physical homes for birds and bees or host plants for butterflies. Birds often nest in bird boxes, which can be made specifically for the particular bird you hope to attract. Honeybees, of course, are kept in beehives. For mason and carpenter bees, construct a bee hotel: build a 15- to 30-centimetre-deep frame and fill it with hollow bamboo stems or blocks of wood in which you have drilled holes of varying depths and diameter, ideally 4 to 10 centimetres deep and 2 to 10 millimetres wide.

Planting host plants for butterflies is more challenging. Many native butterflies lay eggs on native trees, shrubs, or wildflowers, not necessarily those that are garden-worthy. Native butterfly caterpillars often feed upon willows.

Many birds eat berries, particularly serviceberry, holly, cotoneaster, and viburnum. Refer to Shrubs and vines at a glance (page 35) for shrubs and vines that attract wildlife.

Cotoneaster is a favourite of fruit-eating birds.

Gardens of note in Atlantic Canada

- Memorial University of Newfoundland Botanical Garden, 306 Mount Scio Road, St. John's, Newfoundland. Key display: perennials, rhododendrons, heritage plants, rock gardens.

- Bowring Park, 305 Waterford Bridge Road, St. John's, Newfoundland. Key display: annuals, trees, shrubs.

- Halifax Public Gardens, 5664 Spring Garden Road, Halifax, Nova Scotia. Key display: perennials, annuals, trees, shrubs.

- Annapolis Royal Historic Gardens, 441 St. George Street, Annapolis Royal, Nova Scotia. Key display: perennials, roses, heritage plants.

- Harriet Irving Botanical Gardens, 32 University Avenue, Wolfville, Nova Scotia. Key display: native plants.

- Tangled Garden, 11827 Highway 1, Grand Pré, Nova Scotia. Key display: labyrinth, arbours, perennials.

- Bible Hill Rock Garden, Dalhousie Agricultural Campus, College Road, Bible Hill, Nova Scotia. Key display: rock gardens, trees, shrubs.

- New Brunswick Botanical Garden, 15 Rue Principale, Saint-Jacques, New Brunswick. Key display: perennials, annuals, trees, shrubs, rock garden, roses.

- Irving Arboretum, 52 Couvent Way, Bouctouche, New Brunswick. Key display: trees.

- Kingsbrae Garden, 220 King Street, Saint Andrews, New Brunswick. Key display: perennials, annuals, rhododendrons, roses.

- A.A. MacDonald Memorial Gardens, Glenelg Street East, Georgetown, Prince Edward Island. Key display: perennials, annuals, trees, shrubs.

Tangled Garden, Nova Scotia.

Shrubs and vines at a glance

SHRUBS AND VINES FOR COLD, EXPOSED SITES
Arctostaphylos uva-ursi – Bearberry
Aronia – Chokeberry
Cornus alba – Red-osier dogwood
Cotoneaster acutifolius – Peking cotoneaster
Daphne mezereum – February daphne
Hippophae rhamnoides – Sea buckthorn
Hydrangea paniculata – Peegee hydrangea
Juniperus – Juniper
Larix – Larch
Philadelphus – Mock-orange
Physocarpus – Ninebark
Picea – Spruce
Pinus – Pine
Potentilla – Potentilla
Ribes alpinum – Alpine currant
Salix – Willow
Spiraea – Spirea
Viburnum opulus – Highbush cranberry

SHRUBS AND VINES FOR SEASIDE GARDENS
Arctostaphylos uva-ursi – Bearberry
Cotoneaster – Cotoneaster
Cytisus/Genista – Broom

Cytisus X praecox 'Hollandia'.

Hippophae rhamnoides – Sea buckthorn
Juniperus – Juniper
Pinus mugo – Mugo pine
Potentilla – Shrubby cinquefoil
Rosa rugosa – Rugose rose
Salix – Willow
Spiraea – Spirea
Yucca – Yucca

SHRUBS AND VINES FOR SHADE
Akebia quinata – Chocolate vine
Arctostaphylos uva-ursi – Bearberry
Buxus – Boxwood
Celastrus – Bittersweet vine
Gaultheria – Wintergreen
Hedera – English ivy
Hydrangea anomala – Climbing hydrangea
Leucothöe – Fetterbush
Mahonia aquifolium – Oregon-grape
Pachysandra – Japanese spurge
Parthenocissus – Virginia creeper/Boston ivy
Ribes alpinum – Alpine currant
Schizophragma hydrangeoides – Japanese climbing hydrangea
Skimmia japonica – Japanese skimmia
Symphoricarpos – Snowberry
Taxus – Yew
Tsuga canadensis – Eastern hemlock

SHRUBS AND VINES FOR DAMP SITES
Amelanchier – Serviceberry
Aronia – Chokeberry
Clethra alnifolia – Spicebush
Cornus alba – Red-osier dogwood
Physocarpus – Ninebark
Salix – Willow
Sambucus – Elderberry
Sorbaria sorbifolia – Ural false spirea
Symphoricarpos – Snowberry
Thuja occidentalis – Eastern white cedar
Viburnum opulus – Highbush cranberry

Erica carnea 'Myretoun Ruby'.

SHRUBS AND VINES FOR DRY, ACIDIC SOIL
Acer ginnala – Amur maple
Berberis – Barberry
Calluna vulgaris – Heather
Caragana – Peashrub
Cotoneaster – Cotoneaster
Cytisus/Genista – Broom
Elaeagnus angustifolia – Russian olive
Erica – Heath
Juniperis – Junipers
Kerria japonica – Japanese kerria
Lonicera – Honeysuckle
Physocarpus – Ninebark
Pinus – Pine
Tamarix – Salt-cedar

ERICACEOUS SHRUBS FOR ACIDIC SOIL
Andromeda glaucophylla – Bog rosemary
Arctostaphylos uva-ursi – Bearberry
Calluna vulgaris – Heather
Cassiope – Bell heather
Daboecia cantabrica – St. Dabeoc's heath
Enkianthus – Enkianthus
Gaultheria – Wintergreen
Leiophyllum buxifolium – Sand-myrtle
Leucothöe – Fetterbush
Pernettya mucronata – Prickly heath
Pieris – Japanese andromeda

Kalmia latifolia – Mountain laurel
Phyllodoce – Mountain heather
Rhododendron – Rhododendron and azalea
X *Phylliopsis* – Phylliopsis
Zenobia pulverulenta – Honey-cup

SHRUBS AND VINES FOR ALKALINE SOIL
Berberis – Barberry
Buddleja – Butterfly-bush
Buxus – Boxwood
Caragana – Peashrub
Cotoneaster – Cotoneaster
Deutzia – Deutzia
Elaeagnus angustifolia – Russian olive
Euonymous – Euonymus, burning bush
Forsythia – Forsythia
Hypericum – St. John's-wort
Juniperus – Junipers
Lavendula – Lavender
Ligustrum – Privet
Lonicera – Honeysuckle
Philadelphus – Mock-orange

Syringa vulgaris 'Madame Lemoine'.

Pinus – Pines
Potentilla – Shrubby cinquefoil
Rhus – Sumac
Rosa – Roses
Sambucus – Elderberry
Spiraea – Spirea
Symphoricarpos – Snowberry
Syringa – Lilac
Thuja occidentalis – Eastern white cedar
Thujopsis dolobrata – Hiba arborvitae
Weigela – Weigela
Yucca – Yucca

SHRUBS WITH DECORATIVE WINTER BARK
Cornus alba – Red-osier dogwood
Corylus avellana 'Contorta' – Corkscrew hazel
Kerria japonica – Japanese kerria
Salix 'Flame' – Flame willow

SHRUBS AND VINES FOR FALL FOLIAGE
Acer – Dwarf maple
Actinidia – Kiwi
Amelanchier – Serviceberry
Ampeliopsis – Porcelain vine
Aronia – Chokeberry
Berberis thunbergii – Barberry
Celastrus – Bittersweet vine
Clethra – Summersweet
Cornus alba – Red-osier dogwood
Cotoneaster – Cotoneaster
Enkianthus – Enkianthus
Euonymus alatus – Burning bush
Fothergilla – Fothergilla
Hamamelis – Chinese witch-hazel
Larix – Larch
Parthenocissus – Virginia creeper/Boston ivy
Rhododendron – Azalea
Rhus – Sumac
Stephanandra – Lace shrub
Viburnum – Viburnum
Vitis – Grape

Daphne cneorum.

SHRUBS AND VINES
WITH FRAGRANT FLOWERS
Akebia quinata – Chocolate vine
Buddleja – Butterfly-bush
Clethra – Summersweet
Corylopsis – Winter hazel
Daphne – Daphne
Deutzia – Deutzia
Elaeagnus – Russian olive
Fothergilla – Fothergilla
Hamamelis – Chinese witch-hazel
Heptacodium miconoides – Seven-son flower
Itea – Sweetspire
Lavendula – Lavender
Ligustrum – Privet
Lindera benzoin – Spicebush
Lonicera caprifolium/periclymenum – Honeysuckle vine
Magnolia – Magnolia
Philadelphus – Mock-orange
Rhododendron – Deciduous azalea
Ribes aureum – Golden currant
Rosa – Roses
Syringa – Lilac
Viburnum – Fragrant snowball
Wisteria – Wisteria

TODD BOLAND

Lavendula angustifolia 'Munstead'.

Shrubs and Vines for Wildlife

Amelanchier – Serviceberry
Aronia – Chokeberry
Buddleja – Butterfly-bush
Campsis radicans – Trumpetcreeper
Caryopteris – Bluebeard
Clethra – Summersweet
Cotoneaster – Cotoneaster
Hibiscus syriacus – Rose-of-Sharon
Hydrangea paniculata – Peegee hydrangea
Ilex – Holly
Lavendula – Lavender
Lonicera – Honeysuckle
Philadelphus – Mock-orange
Potentilla – Shrubby cinquefoil
Pyracantha coccinea – Firethorn
Rhododendron – Rhododendron
Ribes aureum – Golden currant
Rosa – Rose
Sambucus – Elderberry
Spiraea – Spirea
Viburnum – Viburnum
Vitis – Grape
Weigela – Weigela

Best Deer-/Moose-Resistant Shrubs and Vines

Berberis – Barberry
Buddleja – Butterfly-bush
Buxus – Boxwood
Callicarpa – Beautyberry
Campsis radicans – Trumpet creeper
Caryopteris – Bluebeard
Celastrus – Bittersweet vine
Chamaecyparis – False cypress
Euonymus fortunei – Wintercreeper
Forsythia – Forsythia
Juniperus – Juniper
Kolkwitzia amabilis – Beautybush
Lavendula – Lavender
Lonicera – Honeysuckle
Mahonia aquifolium – Oregon-grape holly
Microbiota – Siberian cypress
Morella pensylvanica – Bayberry
Picea – Spruce
Potentilla – Shrubby cinquefoil
Sambucus – Elderberry
Spiraea – Spirea
Syringa – Lilac
Viburnum – Viburnum (any with fuzzy leaves)
Weigela – Weigela
Wisteria – Wisteria

Weigela florida 'Variegata'.

Symphoricarpos albus.

Shrubs for hedging

Berberis thunbergii – Japanese barberry
Buxus – Boxwood
Cotoneaster acutifolius – Peking cotoneaster
Ligustrum – Privet
Ribes alpinum – Alpine currant
Symphoricarpos – Snowberry
Taxus – Yew

Acer palmatum
JAPANESE MAPLE

Japanese maple are among the most desirable of garden trees and shrubs. As a wild species, Japanese maple is a small tree that can reach 8 metres. Although they have single stems, several cultivars are less than 2 metres when mature and appear more like, and blend well with, shrubs. The weeping forms, if low-grafted, often appear shrublike, with mounded or rounded habits. Popular cultivars include 'Waterfall' (green, yellow in fall), 'Viridis' (green, orange-red in fall), 'Crimson Queen' (purple, red in fall), 'Inaba shidare' (purple, red in fall), and 'Garnet' (purple, red in fall). These are particularly attractive when planted atop a retaining wall.

A few recommended upright dwarf shrubby Japanese maples include 'Beni Hime' (red-tinted in summer, red in fall), 'Coonara Pygmy' (green, multicoloured in fall), 'Sharp's Pygmy' (green, red in fall), 'Shishigashima' (green, orange in fall), and 'Wilsons Pink Dwarf' (pink new foliage, pinkish red in fall). These are often planted as a stand-alone plant, along foundations, in large rockeries, or as patio container plants.

Japanese maple need full sun to part shade and shelter—wind can cause leaf-tip browning in summer or stem dieback in winter. The soil should be well drained, fertile, and acidic. Japanese maple do not tolerate drought or salt. Leafrollers and Japanese beetle are the most frequent insect pests. Canker, wilts, and leaf spot can be troublesome. Larger browsers relish Japanese maple in winter. Propagation is by grafting. They are rated hardy to warmer areas of zone 5.

PREVIOUS SPREAD: *Buxus* 'Green Gem'.
Acer palmatum 'Red Dragon'.

Amelanchier
SERVICEBERRY, JUNEBERRY, SHADBLOW

About 20 species of *Amelanchier*, along with naturally occurring hybrids, are available. A number of them are native to Atlantic Canada. Most are medium to large multi-stemmed deciduous shrubs but some are trained as small trees. Heights range from 2 to 10 metres. The leaves are typically oval to elliptical, with most turning shades of yellow, orange, and red in autumn. The white flowers, produced in May or June, are in terminal clusters or racemes of 2 to 20 flowers and are appreciated by early emerging bees. Flowers later develop into sweet, juicy, purple-black berrylike pomes.

Among the multi-stemmed, shrubby types, highly recommended are *A. spicata*, which reaches 1.2 metres; *A. stolonifera*, 2 metres; *A. bartramiana*, 2.5 metres; and the hybrid 'La Paloma', with outstanding bronzy purple spring growth, 2 to 4 metres.

Amelanchier spicata.
BELOW: *Amelanchier laevis.*

Saskatoon berry, *Amelanchier alnifolia*, is a large shrub that reaches 6 metres but is more commonly less than 4 metres. There are many named cultivars on the market. The above shrubby types are ideal for borders or for naturalizing under taller deciduous trees. They are also ideal for an edible garden.

Amelanchier are best grown in organic-rich, evenly moist soil. Some tolerate very wet, acidic soil, lending themselves for use along wet depressions, pond margins, or streamsides. The exception is Saskatoon berry, which is better adapted to dry, alkaline soil. Full sun produces the most flowers, fruit, and best fall colour, but it tolerates part shade. Propagation is by seed or summer cuttings.

Amelanchier are prone to powdery mildew, fungal spotting, fire blight, and a rust that can attack the developing fruit. Several moth species as well as leaf miners can attack them. They may occasionally be browsed by deer and moose. They are hardy to zone 4; *A. alnifolia* is rated for zone 2.

Aralia
Devil's walking-stick, angelica tree

Most of the popular *Aralia* are herbaceous perennials, but two woody types are grown in Atlantic Canada. From China, Japan, and eastern Siberia comes angelica tree, *A. elata*, while from the eastern US comes devil's walking-stick, *A. spinosa*. Both form multi-stemmed large shrubs 3 to 5 metres tall. Typically, they have few branches and extremely spiny stems. Their 60- to 120-centimetre-long, fernlike, compound leaves impart a tropical effect. The undersides of the leaves of angelica tree are pubescent; those of devil's walking stick are mostly smooth. Fall colour varies from yellow to shades of red. In late summer to early fall it produces large 45-centimetre-long sprays of tiny white flowers that at-

Aralia spinosa.

tract bees. Flowers may later develop into small black fruit relished by fruit-eating birds.

Generally, these woody *Aralia* are easy to grow in any well-drained site in full sun or part shade. As they can sucker aggressively, they are perhaps best used in a naturalized setting, unless you judiciously remove unwanted suckers. Insects are not a problem, but some fungal leaf spot problems may arise. Handling the plant can cause dermatitis in sensitive-skinned people. Propagation is by removing the suckers, which can then be planted as new plants. Both are hardy to zone 4.

Aronia melanocarpa.

Aronia
CHOKEBERRY

There are three species of *Aronia*, all native to eastern North America, including Atlantic Canada. They are deciduous shrubs with spoon-shaped leaves that turn brilliant shades of orange, red, and purple in autumn. Clusters of white flowers with pink stamens are produced in late spring, becoming clusters of edible, albeit tasteless, berries in the fall. Their flowers are attractive to bees, and their berries to birds. Red chokeberry, *A. arbutifolia*, is the tallest, reaching 4 metres. Its leaves are white and pubescent on their undersides, and the fruit are bright red. Black chokeberry, *A. melanocarpa*, grows 1.5 to 2 metres, has leaves with smooth undersides, and berries that become black. Purple chokeberry, *A.* X *prunifolia*, is a hybrid between the former two and appears like a smaller version of the black chokeberry. The berries of all three often remain on the bushes all winter, adding winter interest. There are three suggested selections of black chokeberry. 'Autumn Magic' was selected for its intense orange-red fall colour, while Iroquois Beauty™ was selected for both its wonderful fall colour and more compact 1-metre habit.

Low Scape®, a dwarf selection, reaches just 60 centimetres. 'Brilliantissima', a selection of red chokeberry, has the best red fall colour, abundant fruit, and a compact 2-metre habit. Use chokeberry in mixed shrub borders and naturalized areas or along stream- or lakesides.

Chokeberries prefer organic-rich, evenly moist soil. They are also suitable for boggy, acidic sites but are not well adapted to dry areas. Full sun produces the heaviest fruit set and best fall colour. Propagation is by summer cuttings or seed. Few pests or diseases bother them, although pear slugs are occasional pests. Black chokeberry is hardy to zone 3; the red and purple are rated for zone 4.

Aronia melanocarpa 'Autumn Magic'.

TODD BOLAND

Artemisia abrotanum.

Artemisia
SOUTHERNWOOD, BOY'S-LOVE

Most *Artemisia* are herbaceous perennials, but several are woody, such as sagebrush, *A. tridentata*. In Atlantic Canada a single species is sometimes encountered. Commonly known as southernwood, *Artemisia abrotanum* is known in Newfoundland as boy's-love. This plant has been grown in Atlantic Canada for over 100 years; hence, it has heirloom or heritage status as a garden plant. It is rarely sold by nurseries, yet it still exists, as it is easy to raise from cuttings. Plants form rounded mounds to 120 centimetres with soft, ferny, silvery green foliage that is strongly aromatic. It rarely flowers in Atlantic Canada. With age it can get leggy and scruffy, but with regular pruning, it can form an attractive shrub. It may be used as an accent but is more commonly positioned near walkways, where its fragrant foliage can be best appreciated. It may also be used as a low, informal hedge. The dried leaves may be used in potpourri and sachets.

Southernwood prefer full sun and organic-rich soil that is well drained. Its drought and salt tolerance makes it useful in coastal gardens. However, it does not tolerate wet soil. In the wild, it usually occurs on limestone rock; in the garden, a regular dusting of lime is beneficial. It is generally pest and disease free and easily propagated by summer cuttings. It is rated hardy to zone 4.

Berberis
BARBERRY

Most of the nearly 450 species of barberry are native to South America, including both broad-leaved evergreen and deciduous species. All have one feature in common: many spines located

Berberis thunbergii 'Sunsation'.

Berberis thunbergii 'Helmund Pillar'.

along the length of their stems. The leaves are simple, ovate to elliptical, and generally smooth-edged on deciduous species, while toothed and often spiny on the evergreen types. Small yellow to orange flowers, produced in May and into June, are either solitary or in drooping racemes. The flowers later develop into teardrop-shaped berries, which are often red on deciduous species and blue on the evergreen. Barberry are closely related to *Mahonia*, the grape-hollies.

The most popular species is the deciduous Japanese barberry, *Berberis thunbergii*. It has enjoyed a resurgence in popularity in recent years and numerous selections have been released. While the species may reach 2 to 3 metres, many of the newer cultivars are less than 1.5 metres. The purple-leaved forms are perhaps the most popular, but yellow, orange, and variegated forms are also available. Over 50 cultivars are on the market, including 'Rose Glow' (purple leaves mottled with pink and white, 2 metres), 'Harlequin' (similar to 'Rose Glow', but 1.5 metres), Royal Burgundy® (purple, 1 metre), 'Concorde' (dark purple, 75 centimetres), Cherry Bomb® (bright purple, 1 metre), 'Crimson Pygmy' (purple, 1 metre), 'Helmund Pillar' (purple, 1.5 metres, narrow habit), Golden Ruby® (orange-purple, 60 centimetres), Sunjoy® Tangelo (orange-pink with golden edge, 1.2 metres), Sunsation® (yellow, 1.2 metres), 'Aurea Nana' (yellow, 90 centimetres), Golden Nugget™ (yellow, 30 centimetres), Sunjoy Gold Pillar™ (yellow, 1.2 metres, narrow habit), 'Lime Glow' (chartreuse, 1.5 metres), and 'Kobold' (green, fruitless, 60 centimetres). Many of these have superb fall colours in shades of yellow, orange, and red.

Among the evergreen types, the most popular are *B. verruculosa* (yellow flowers, 2 metres),

Berberis julianae.

B. gagnepainii (yellow, 2.4 metres), and *B. julianae* (yellow, 2.4 metres). All of these have small hollylike foliage with whitened undersides and blue fruit.

Barberry are generally care-free and easy to grow in full sun to part shade and any well-drained soil. They are also drought- and, in the case of Japanese barberry, salt-tolerant. Barberry are popular as foundation plants or hedging, or as accents in a shrub border. Japanese barberry is also highly suited for coastal gardens. Pests and diseases are rare. Propagation is by summer cuttings or seed, but named selections may not come true to form if grown from seed. Japanese barberry is hardy to zone 4. The evergreen species are less hardy: *B. verruculosa* and *B. gagnepainii*, zone 5, and *B. julianae*, zone 6.

Buddleja
Butterfly-bush

The genus *Buddleja* was named in honour of Revered Adam Buddle (1662–1715), an English botanist and rector. While there are now over 140 species, *B. davidii*, a species native to China, is seen most often in Atlantic Canada. It has been grown as a garden ornamental since the 1890s. With such a long period of cultivation, numerous cultivars are available. The wild butterfly-bush, an upright shrub with arching branches, reaches 3 to 5 metres. Paired lance-shaped leaves are grey-green and pubescent. In late summer through fall, the branch tips end in dense panicles of numerous small, fragrant, lilac to purple flowers, with characteristic yellow eyes. Each panicle may be 20 centimetres or more in length, resulting in a magnificent display of late-season flowers. As the common name suggests, flowers are relished by butterflies, but also by hummingbirds and bees.

Today's modern cultivars are available in shades of pink, purple, red, and lavender-blue, as well as white. Popular are 'Black Knight', 'White Profusion', 'Pink Delight', 'Royal Red', 'Cornwall Blue', 'White Bouquet', and the 'Nanho' and 'Buzz' series. These all reach 2 to 3 metres. For something different, try 'Harlequin' (violet-red) or 'Summer Skies' (lavender-blue), both of which have decorative white-margined leaves. Butterfly-bush are often grown at the back of

Buddleja davidii 'Pink Delight'.

Buddleja Adonis Blue™.

perennial borders or among cottage gardens. If space is an issue, try one of several dwarf butterfly-bush hybrids on the market toward the front of a shrub border or along foundations. Adonis Blue™ is a compact hybrid 100-175 centimetres while Lo and Behold® 'Blue Chip' is a grey-leaved hybrid with lavender-blue flowers on 75- to 100-centimetre-tall plants. Other Lo and Behold® hybrids are available in pink and purple.

Butterfly-bush are lovers of sun and summer heat, performing best in warm inland areas. They are drought-tolerant but do not tolerate wet sites. Pests and diseases are not an issue nor are they bothered by larger browsers. Propagation is by summer or hardwood cuttings. While rated hardy to zone 5, they often suffer severe dieback in winter. If this occurs, simply hard-prune. Butterfly-bush flower on new wood, so even when cut back hard, they often bloom quite well.

Buxus
BOXWOOD

The majority of the 70 species of boxwood are tropical species. In Atlantic Canada we grow *Buxus sempervirens*, *B. microphylla*, and their hybrids. The former species can reach 3 to 5 metres in the wild; the latter is dwarf, at about 1 metre. Generally, in the garden, boxwood are either pruned to less than 1 metre or the cultivars naturally stay dwarf. Both the species and the hybrids have small, evergreen, glossy green, elliptical leaves that often take on bronzy tints in winter. They produce insignificant yellow-green axillary flowers in May. The most popular cultivars are

Buxus 'Green Gem'.

Callicarpa dichotoma 'Early Amethyst'.

'Green Gem' (75 centimetres, globular), 'Green Mound' (100 centimetres, globular), 'Green Velvet' (100 centimetres, globular), North Star® (80 centimetres, globular), Sprinter® (120 centimetres, upright), 'Green Mountain' (150 centimetres, upright), and Green Tower™ (250 centimetres). The upright forms are best for hedging; the globular are popular as foundation or container plants. Variegated boxwoods—*B. sempervirens* 'Variegata' (150 centimetres), whose leaves are edged in white, and 'Golden Triumph', whose leaves are narrowly edged in yellow—are also available.

Boxwood grow in sun or shade as long as the soil is reasonably fertile and well drained. However, full sun in winter can cause the foliage to become bronzy; too much shade results in a loose habit. As winter burn is common, provide a sheltered location. Boxwood are reasonably drought-tolerant once established. Diseases are not common, but in warmer areas watch for leaf miners. Propagation is by fall cuttings. Boxwood are rated hardy to zone 5, but with good winter protection can survive in zone 4. 'Green Velvet' is considered the hardiest cultivar.

Callicarpa dichotoma
Beautyberry

Of over 100 species of *Callicarpa*, only one is grown in Atlantic Canada: *C. dichotoma*, a species native to China, Japan, and Korea. A sprawling shrub up to 1.2 metres tall, its stems are arching, often touching the ground. Paired elliptical leaves turn golden yellow in autumn. In midsummer plants produce axillary clusters of tiny pale pink flowers that develop into stunning violet berries in October. For best results, prune plants back to 15 centimetres in spring. This keeps them compact and encourages fruiting stems. To maximize fruit production, plant beautyberry in groups. 'Early Amethyst' is the best cultivar for Atlantic Canada. It is among the best shrubs for fruit display and useful for the front of a shrub border or along foundations.

Beautyberry prefer full sun and any well-drained soil. Pests and diseases are rare, but as it is prone to severe dieback in cold winters, a sheltered site is recommended. Propagation is by summer cuttings. It is rated hardy to zone 5, but as it is a heat-lover, it performs better in the Maritimes, rarely setting fruit in Newfoundland.

Caragana
PEASHRUB

All 100 species of *Caragana* are native to northern Asia and Eastern Europe. Despite the large number of species, only two are commonly grown as a garden ornamental in Atlantic Canada: the Siberian peashrub, *C. arborescens*; and pygmy peashrub, *C. pygmaea*. The former is a 2- to 6-metre-tall coarse shrub featuring small pinnate leaves with round leaflets, short spines, and solitary or small clusters of 2-centimetre-diameter yellow, pealike flowers in late spring or early summer. 'Sutherland' was selected for its narrower, columnar form. 'Lorbergii' has narrow leaflets that impart a feathery look to the foliage. The two weeping forms of peashrub are top-grafted at 1.5 to 2 metres; their branches sweep to the ground. 'Pendula' has standard peashrub foliage, while 'Walker' has narrow leaflets similar to those of 'Lorbergii'. Pygmy peashrub, *C. pygmaea*, has small elliptical leaflets in tufts and solitary yellow flowers, can reach 1.2 metres, and has a rounded habit.

Siberian peashrub is a tough, adaptable plant that tolerates poor, dry soil, windy sites, and even roadside and coastal salt, but it does not tolerate wet soil. The standard peashrub is too coarse for most gardens, but it is useful as a living screen or windbreak. 'Lorbergii', a little more ornamental, can be used in the back of a shrub border. The weeping forms are often used for foundations, as a specimen, or in a shrub border. They blend well with conifers; try combining with an evergreen backdrop. Peashrub is an excellent candidate for a seaside garden. Propagation is by seed, grafting, or summer cuttings. Peashrub is not bothered by pests or diseases. Hardy to zone 2, it may be grown throughout Atlantic Canada.

Caragana arborescens 'Pendula'.

Caryopteris X *clandonensis*
BLUEBEARD

Popular as a container or bedding plant, *Caryopteris* X *clandonensis* can be hardy in warmer areas of the Maritimes. The genus originates from East Asia; the hybrid is most often grown as a garden ornamental. Plants can reach 90 centimetres, with paired, lance-shaped, aromatic foliage. Tiny fluffy blue flowers are produced in the upper leaf axils from August to October. The most popular cultivars are 'Dark Knight' and 'Worchester Gold', the latter having golden

Caryopteris X *cladonensis* 'Dark Knight'.

yellow foliage which contrasts beautifully with the blue flowers. Bluebeard, often grown as a container plant, in a flower border, or along the front of shrub borders, attracts bees and butterflies.

Bluebeard need a warm, sunny spot with well-drained soil; sandy soils are ideal. It is impervious to pests and disease but wet winter soil causes root rot. Propagation is by summer cuttings. While rated hardy to zone 5, bluebeard usually dies back severely in winter and is treated as an herbaceous perennial. Since it blooms on new wood, cutting plants back to the ground each spring does not usually negatively impact blooming. Bluebeard is a difficult shrub to accommodate in Newfoundland, as the summers are not hot enough.

Cephalanthus occidentalis
BUTTONBUSH

Rarely seen in Atlantic Canada but a worthwhile shrub for naturalized settings is buttonbush, *Cephalanthus occidentalis*, a native of southeastern North America. This deciduous shrub can reach 3 to 4 metres tall. The waxy, elliptical leaves are relatively late to unfurl. Flowers are produced in open clusters at the tips of the stems from midsummer onward. Individual flowers are tiny, white, and fragrant, but are held in 3-centimetre-diameter spherical heads. The exerted stamens and pistils give the flowers a pincushion appearance. The genus name comes from the Greek words *cephalo*, head, and *anthos*, flower, a reference to the unique inflorescence. The flowers are frequently visited by bees and butterflies. In autumn, the faded flower heads become spherical red balls that remain on the shrub all winter. Magical® Moonlight is a smaller cultivar reaching 1.7 metres; Sugar Shack® is dwarf, reaching 1.2 metres. 'Sputnik', at 3 metres, was selected for its shell pink flowers.

Buttonbush prefer full sun to part shade and a damp, organic-rich soil. It can tolerate standing water for short periods of time. As a result, it is ideal for damp depressions or along water features. It does not tolerate any degree of drought. Overall, it is a care-free shrub, with few pests or diseases. Propagation is by seed or summer cuttings. It is rated hardy to zone 5.

Cephalanthus occidentalis.

Chaenomeles X *superba* 'Crimson and Gold'.

Chaenomeles
FLOWERING QUINCE

Flowering quince are among the most colourful spring-blooming shrubs. As ornamentals, Atlantic Canadian gardeners grow Japanese quince, *Chaenomeles japonica*, Chinese quince, *C. speciosus*, and hybrids referred to as *C.* X *superba*. Flowering quince are broad-spreading shrubs. Their height, depending on the cultivar, ranges from 1 to 3.5 metres. While their glossy deciduous leaves are charming in summer, they have no appreciable fall colour. All have spines, making them effective barriers. The single or double apple-blossom-like flowers are produced in clusters, primarily in May, just before or as the leaves appear. Flowers are in shades of pink, red, orange, or white. Later in the summer, flowers become small crabapple-like fruit. While not edible in a raw state, they can be used for making preserves. Suggested cultivars include 'Crimson and Gold' (crimson red), 'Rowallane' (dark crimson), 'Nicoline' (deep red), 'Texas Scarlet' (bright red), 'Pink Lady' (deep pink), 'Coral Sea' (light pink), 'Pink Storm' (double pink), 'Orange Storm' (double orange), 'Cameo' (semi-double light orange), and 'Jet Trail' (white).

Flowering quince perform best with slightly acidic soil; too high pH can lead to chlorosis of the leaves. While these plants prefer fertile, well-drained, evenly moist soil, they tolerate brief periods of drought. Full sun produces the most flowers but part shade is tolerated. The taller cultivars of flowering quince may be used as informal hedging. Otherwise, they may be used in a mixed shrub border. They also lend themselves to use in cottage gardens and edible landscapes. Propagation is by summer cuttings. Typical of most members of the rose family, flowering quince may be bothered by a host of pests and diseases. Aphids, scale, pear slug, and leafrollers are the main insect pests, while fungal leaf spotting and fireblight are the main diseases. Because they are early blooming, avoid low-lying frost pockets. Chinese quince is hardy to zone 4, while Japanese quince and the hybrids are better in zones 5 or warmer.

NEXT PAGE: *Chaenomeles* X *superba* 'Cameo'.

Clethra

SUMMERSWEET, SWEET PEPPERBUSH

The genus name *Clethra* comes from the Greek *klethra*, alder, in reference to the alderlike appearance of the plants. Two main species of *Clethra* are grown as garden ornamentals: the North American summersweet, *Clethra alnifolia*, a rare Atlantic Coastal plain species found in southwestern Nova Scotia; and Japanese clethra, *C. barbinervis*, from China, Korea, and Japan. Both are deciduous, multi-stemmed, suckering shrubs. Their leaves are lance-shaped, distinctly veined with finely toothed edges. The fall colour is typically yellow. Fragrant flowers are produced in narrow, bottlebrush-like racemes during late summer and into autumn. Flowers are white or, less commonly, pink.

Summersweet is more popular than Japanese clethra, probably due to its smaller, hardier nature. The wild form of summersweet reaches 2.4 metres, with 10- to 15-centimetre-long, fragrant flower spikes. Named selections include 'Hummingbird', which is compact and floriferous, topping at 1 metre; 'Sixteen Candles', which has erect flowers on 1.2-metre plants; Vanilla Spice™, whose flower spikes are up to 30 centimetres long; 'Pink Spire', with light pink flowers; and 'Ruby Spice', whose flowers are rose pink. Einstein™ has twisted flower stems, resulting in flowers that are white and wild like Einstein's hair. Japanese clethra, more challenging to find, generally grows much taller, reaching 3 to 6 metres. Its exfoliating bark is quite striking. Its less fragrant flower spikes are generally held more horizontal than those of summersweet.

All *Clethra* prefer acidic soil that is evenly moist and well drained. Summersweet tolerates quite wet soil. They flower best in full sun. Use *Clethra* as foundation plants, in a mixed shrub border, in naturalized areas, or as understory shrubs beneath tall deciduous trees. With its love of water, summersweet also lends itself to use along water features. Overall, *Clethra* are care-free plants, with few insect or disease problems. Propagation may be by seed or more commonly by summer cuttings. Summersweet is hardy to zone 3, while Japanese clethra is rated for zone 5.

Clethra alnifolia 'Pink Spice'.

Clethra alnifolia.

Cornus
DOGWOOD

Thirty to 60 species of dogwood are found throughout the northern hemisphere, ranging from low-growing woodlanders like the native bunchberry, *Cornus canadensis*, to small trees like Chinese flowering dogwood, *C. kousa*, which can reach 10 metres. The genus name comes from the Latin word *cornu*, horn, a reference to the strength of the wood.

The most popular shrubby dogwood is the red-osier or red-twig dogwood, *C. sericea*, also known in the literature as *C. stolonifera*, *C. siberica*, *C. sanguinea*, and *C. alba*. This shrub, which is native to Atlantic Canada, will reach 1 to 3 metres and was traditionally grown for its red stems, which show in winter. However, they do produce flat-topped clusters of white flowers in late May or June, followed by white or pale blue berries in autumn. Elliptical leaves typically turn a mix of yellow, orange, and red in autumn. Among the popular red-stemmed cultivars are 'Baileyi' (3 metres), 'Cardinal' (2.8 metres), 'Isanti' (1.8 metres), 'Midwinter Fire' (1.8 metres), 'Prairie Fire' (1.8 metres), Arctic Fire® (1.8 metres), Little Rebel™ (1.25 metres), Firedance™ (1.2 metres), and 'Kelseyi' (0.8 metres). Yellow-twigged selections include 'Flaviramia' (2.8 metres), 'Bud's Yellow' (2.8 metres), and Arctic Sun® (1.8 metres). With white-edged foliage are 'Elegantissima' (3 metres, red stems), 'Silver and Gold' (2.7 metres, yellow stems), Ivory Halo® (1.7 metres, red stems), and Crème de Mint™ (1.7 metres, green stems). With yellow-edged leaves are 'Gouchaulti' (3 metres, red stems) and 'Hedgerow Gold' (1.8 metres, red stems). Finally, with completely yellow foliage are 'Prairie Fire' (2.5 metres, red stems) and Neon Burst™ (1.5 metres, red stems).

Cornus alba 'Elegantissima'.

Cornus alba 'Midwinter Fire'.

Red-osier dogwoods do well in full sun to full shade, but the best flowering and foliage colour is in full sun. Any reasonably fertile soil will do as long as it is evenly moist. Dogwoods are moisture-lovers and grow particularly well in damp depressions or along water features. They are also popular as foundation shrubs or in mixed shrub borders and particularly valued for their winter display. The most common insect problem is leaf miners; fungal spotting, tip blight, and powdery mildew are commonly encountered diseases. Be forewarned that deer and moose love to browse dogwood. Propagation is primarily by either summer or hardwood cuttings. As red-osier dogwood is hardy to zone 3, it may be grown throughout Atlantic Canada.

Corylopsis
WINTER HAZEL

All 30 species of *Corylopsis* are native to eastern Asia. The genus name translates from the Greek as hazel-like, in reference to the foliage. As a group, *Corylopsis* are broad-spreading deciduous shrubs with ovate, sharply toothed, distinctly veined leaves that turn yellow in autumn. The flowers are lemon yellow, bell-like, and produced in nodding clusters before the leaves unfurl in May. Most are lightly fragrant. Perhaps the most impressive for flowers and fragrance is *C. spicata*, which can reach 3 metres tall and 4 or more metres wide. It can have up to 12 flowers on 5-centimetre-long racemes. 'Golden Spring' is a beautiful yellow-foliaged selection; 'Variegata' has irregular streaks and patches of white. Similar to *C. spicata* is *C. glabrescens*, which is also quite fragrant. 'Lemon Drop', a smaller selection, tops at 2 metres. *Corylopsis chinensis* is taller than the previous two species, reaching to 5 metres, and its flowers are only lightly fragrant but in denser clusters. 'Spring Purple' has purple-tinted foli-

Corylopsis pauciflora.

age and a fall colour that is a wonderful blend of yellow, orange, red, and purple. *Corylopsis pauciflora* is one of the daintiest species, reaching to 2 metres; its lightly fragrant flowers are produced in small clusters of two to five blossoms on short racemes up to 4 centimetres long.

Corylopsis prefer soil that is evenly moist but well drained, acidic, and humus-rich. Full sun produces the most flowers but part shade is also tolerated. They are not well suited to windy locations. As the early flowers are susceptible to late frosts, avoid frost pockets. *Corylopsis* are related to witch-hazel and *Hamamelis* and combine admirably with them along the borders of a woodland, as an understory beneath tall deciduous trees, or in naturalized areas. Overall, they have few pest or disease issues; however, their horizontal branches make them susceptible to breakage if the snow is deep. Propagation is by summer cuttings or seed. *Corylopsis spictata* and *C. glabrescens* are hardy to zone 5; *C. sinensis* and *C. pauciflora* are tenderer, zone 6, and only suitable for the mildest areas of Nova Scotia.

Corylus
HAZEL

About 15 species of *Corylus* are scattered across the northern hemisphere. The name, from the Greek *korylo*, means helmet, a reference to the shape of the husk surrounding the fruit. All have rounded leaves with distinct ribs and sharp, double-toothed margins. Its fall colour is typically yellow. They grow as medium to large, rounded, sometime suckering shrubs. Plants are monoecious, with separate male and female flowers on the same plant. Female flowers are mostly unnoticeable, but the males are in the form of elongate 5- to 12-centimetre-long catkins that bloom before the leaves unfurl. The fruit, a nut, is edible in some species. Most species naturally grow along the margins of forests, streams, or lakesides, and in the garden, they are useful for similar areas. Only a few species are considered ornamental.

The European hazel, *C. avellana*, is a common hedgerow plant throughout Europe, with four named ornamental selections. 'Contorta', often

Corylus avellana 'Red Dragon'.

called Harry Lauder's walking stick or corkscrew hazel, is a medium shrub to 3 metres. This grafted plant has distinct twisted stems and contorted leaves. 'Red Dragon' and 'Red Majestic' are striking purple-leaved versions. 'Pendula' is a green-leaved, weeping version that is top-grafted and usually grown as a standard. These are all attractive subjects for a winter garden, where their unique shapes can best be appreciated. The commercial filbert or hazelnut is a hybrid of *C. avellana* and *C. maxima* and has many named selections. The native beaked hazelnut, *C. cornuta*, and the American hazel, *C. americana*, both reach 2.5 metres and often grown for their edible nuts, are ideal subjects for an edible landscape.

Hazels perform best under acidic, humus-rich, evenly moist soil conditions. Full sun is best, but they tolerate part shade. In the garden, remove suckers to maintain tidy plants. Pests and disease are not common. Propagation is by grafting or summer cuttings. The above are all hardy to zone 4.

Cotinus coggygria
SMOKEBUSH, SMOKETREE

In the wild, smokebush, *Cotinus coggygria*, is found from southern Europe to central China. It generally forms a large rounded shrub or small tree up to 4.5 metres tall. The blue-green leaves are distinctively round with long petioles. Its fall colour is typically a mix of yellow, orange, and red. The flowers are insignificant but the pink-grey seed heads are large, airy, and fluffy, appearing like puffs of smoke from a distance, giving the plant its common name. Smokebush is popular as a specimen shrub, combined with other shrubs in a mixed border or used as a living screen or informal hedge.

'Daydream', which can reach 3 metres, is the most popular blue-green-leaved selection, while 'Young Lady' is a compact 2-metre-tall selection. Perhaps more popular are the various purple-leaved cultivars. 'Royal Purple', 'Velvet

RIGHT: *Cotinus* 'Grace'.

Cotinus coggygria 'Royal Robe'.

Cotinus coggygria Golden Spirit®.

Cloak', and 'Norcutt's Variety' are quite similar to each other and reach 3 metres, with wine-purple foliage, purple "smoke," and notable red fall foliage. In colder regions, try 'Nordine', which is a little hardier. The leaves of 'Grace', is a hybrid between *C. coggygria* and *C. obovatus*, are a bright purple-red and its fluffy seed heads up to 30 centimetres wide and long. If space is limited, try Winecraft Black®, a dark purple-leaved selection that reaches just 1.5 metres, or Velveteeny™ at 1.2 metres. 'Ancot', also known as Golden Spirit®, has bright yellow summer foliage, and fall colour which is a mix of orange and red. It will reach 3 metres.

Smokebush prefer full sun to develop the best foliage colour and most seed heads. Any soil type is suitable, as long as it is well drained. It performs better in poorer soils than rich. It is very drought-tolerant once established. Pests and diseases are rare, although verticillium wilt can occur. Propagation is by summer cuttings. It is hardy to zone 5, although 'Nordine' may grow in sheltered areas of zone 4.

Cotoneaster
COTONEASTER

Most of the several hundred species of *Cotoneaster* are native to China. Many have highly decorative fruit and, among the deciduous species, excellent fall colour. As a result, they are popular landscape plants, with many species suitable for Atlantic Canada. Some cotoneaster are grown as ground covers on embankments or cascading over retaining walls. Cranberry cotoneaster, *C. apiculatus*, has arching, trailing stems that can reach 100 centimetres tall. Its glossy rounded leaves turn red in autumn. Small pink flowers become showy red fruit. Creeping cotoneaster, *C. adpressus*, is similar but lower-growing at 45 centimetres. Rockspray cotoneaster, *C. horizontalis*, has notable architecture: its stiff lateral branches off the main stems impart a herringbone outline, which is especially evident in winter. Like cranberry cotoneaster, rockspray cotoneaster has glossy, round leaves that turn scarlet in fall. Small pink flowers become bright red decorative fruit. Leaning against a foundation, it can reach

Cotoneaster dammeri.

Cotoneaster horizontalis.

2 metres, but in the open garden it is usually less than 1 metre. 'Perpusillus' is a half-sized version. 'Variegatus' is particularly attractive, with white-margined foliage. Hesse cotoneaster, *C. X hessei*, is a hybrid between *C. horizontalis* and *C. apiculatus* and has the best aspects of both parents.

Atlantic Canada has three main broad-leaved evergreen species, the most popular of which is bearberry cotoneaster, *C. dammeri* 'Coral Beauty'. It has small, glossy, elliptical leaves and showy clusters of white flowers that develop into red fruit that stay on the plants all winter. It can reach 45 centimetres but is fast-spreading through its prostrate branches. It is one of the best ground-cover cotoneasters. 'Lowfast', 'Streibs Findling', and Canadian Creeper™ are even lower, at 30 centimetres. Small-leaved cotoneaster, *C. microphyllus*, has tiny, narrow, shiny green leaves, white flowers, and persistent red fruit on plants reaching 1 metre, but spreads to 2 metres or more. *C. cochleatus* is half the size.

Used primarily as a hedge plant are hedge cotoneaster, *C. lucidus*, and Peking cotoneaster, *C. acutifolius*. The former has glossy, dark green, ovate leaves; the latter, dull green leaves. Both turn shades of yellow, orange, and red in autumn. The pinkish flowers are insignificant and

Cotoneaster lucidus.

develop into indistinct black fruit that often remain through most of the winter. Unclipped, both can reach 3 metres but normally they are maintained as a hedge 60 centimetres to 2 metres tall.

A few other larger 2- to 3-metre-tall cotoneaster shrubs occasionally seen in Atlantic Canada are *C. divaricatus* (glossy leaves, red fall foliage), *C. franchetii* (grey-green semi-evergreen foliage), *C. tomentosus* (grey-green foliage, reddish fall foliage), *C. multiflorus* (glossy leaves, red fall foliage), and *C. bullatus* (waxy green leaves, red fall colour). All of these produce red fruit and, in the case of *C. bullatus*, decorative, persistent clusters that can arch the stems from their weight.

As a group, cotoneaster grow best in full sun and well-drained but fertile soil. They tolerate some shade and a little drought. As cotoneaster are related to apples, cherries, and plums, they are prone to similar pests and diseases, including pear slug, several moth larvae, and fireblight. Overall, they are good bee plants and their fruit are often consumed by birds. Propagation is by summer cuttings or seed. Hardiness varies tremendously. Hedge and Peking cotoneaster are super hardy, zone 2. Cranberry, creeping, rockspray, and Hesse cotoneaster are rated for zone 4. The evergreen, semi-evergreen, and taller shrubs types are rated for zone 5.

Cytisus
Broom

About 50 species of *Cytisus* are found throughout Eurasia, especially around the Mediterranean region. They are closely related and similar to *Genista*. In Atlantic Canada, we grow mostly *C. scoparius*, *C.* X *praecox*, and *C.* X *kewensis*. The former is an upright shrub with green branches and tiny, almost insignificant leaves. It typically reaches 1.5 to 2 metres tall. In June and July, it produces masses of solitary, fragrant, golden yellow pealike flowers along its stems. These later become small pealike pods. In the right location broom can self-seed with abandon and is now naturalized in some parts of Atlantic Canada. 'Moonlight' is a popular pale yellow cultivar. The hybrid *C.* X *praecox* is bushier and more compact than *C. scoparius*, generally less than 1.2 metres tall. 'Allgold' (deep yellow), 'Lena' (orange and red), 'Boskoop Ruby' (pink), and 'Apricot Gem' are the local landscape standards. These are often grown as foundation plants, in mixed shrub borders, or in cottage garden settings. For small

Cytisus scoparius 'Moonlight'.

Cytisus X *kewenensis*.

Daphne
Daphne

All 70-plus species of Daphne are native to Eurasia. While they may be broad-leaved evergreen or deciduous, as a group they are mostly low-stature shrubs with highly fragrant white, yellow, or pink flowers followed by fleshy yellow to red fruit. While several species, including hybrids, are hardy in Atlantic Canada, only a few are likely to be available in local nurseries. Among the most popular is February daphne, *D. mezereum*, which is one of the taller species, reaching 1.2 metres. This species is naturalized in some areas. In April and May, before they leaf, the stems are clothed in reddish pink, stemless flowers. These later become bright red fruit. This is a deciduous species, with leaves turning yellow

gardens and larger rockeries, try *C.* X *kewenensis*, which has a ground-cover-like habit less than 30 centimetres in height. Its flowers are pale yellow.

Broom require sunny, dry sites. Almost any soil type is suitable and it grows reasonably well in poor rocky areas. Pests and diseases are rare. The main concern is root rot in wet situations or winter burn if situated in a windy site. Propagation is by summer cuttings or, in the case of wild *C. scoparius*, seed. The above are all hardy to zone 5, but need some protection from cold winter winds.

Daphne 'Lawrence Crocker'.

Daphne X *burkwoodii* 'Carol Mackie'.

in autumn. 'Bowle's White' is a white-flowered selection with yellow fruit. Another taller daphne, the hybrid *D.* X *burkwoodii*, is usually less than 1 metre, with narrow grey-green spoon-shaped leaves. Technically a semi-evergreen, it is mostly deciduous in Atlantic Canada. Its pale pink flowers are produced as terminal clusters in June but also scattered throughout the summer. 'Somerset' is the standard green-leaved selection; 'Carol Mackie' has creamy yellow-edged leaves. 'Brigg's Moonlight' and 'Lunar Eclipse' have green leaves with yellow centres but are not as reliable in Atlantic Canada as the other *D.* X *burkwoodii* selections.

Also reasonably available is garland daphne, *D. cneorum*, a broad-leaved evergreen with narrow, grey- to blue-green foliage. It generally grows from 30 to 60 centimetres tall. It produces terminal rounded clusters of pink flowers in May-June followed by red berries. 'Ruby Glow' has reddish pink flowers, while 'Variegata' has lovely creamy-edged leaves. 'Lawrence Crocker', a hybrid daphne similar to garland daphne, is less than 30 centimetres; it blooms in May-June but also sporadically through summer. Other daphne to consider are *D.* X *transatlantica* (pale pink, deciduous), *D. alpina* (white, deciduous), *D. caucasica* (white, deciduous), *D. retusa* (pale pink, evergreen), and *D. tangutica* (pale pink, evergreen).

As daphne prefer full sun and neutral to slightly alkaline soil, in most of Atlantic Canada a yearly dusting with lime is beneficial. They tolerate part shade but flowering will not be so prolific. Place daphne near the front of walkways, where their perfume can be best appreciated. The taller types are popular along foundations, and February daphne is even used as an informal hedge. The low types are useful in rock gardens. Excess winter wetness kill them. Daphne, especially the evergreen types, are not fond of windy sites. All daphne are poisonous if ingested. Pests are rare, but daphne are prone to sudden death for no apparent reason, maybe due to viral diseases. Propagation is by seed or summer or fall cuttings. February and garland daphne are rated for zone 4. While *D.* X *burkwoodii* is also listed for zone 4, it is more reliable in zone 5. 'Lawrence Crocker' and the other species or hybrids noted above are rated for zone 5.

Daphne mezereum.

Deutzia
Deutzia

Most of the over 60 species of *Deutzia* are natives of China. The genus name honours Dutch botanist Johan van der Deutz (1743–1788). Only a handful of species are grown in Atlantic Canada. The tallest, *D. scabra*, which can reach 3 metres, produces 7- to 12-centimetre-long spikes of scented, nodding white or pink flowers in June to July. The cultivar 'Candidissima' has double white flowers, while 'Plena' has double pale pink blossoms. A little smaller at 2.5 metres is *D. longifolia* 'Veitchii', which has pink flowers. *Deutzia* X *hybrida* 'Strawberry Fields' has two-tone pink flowers on plants reaching 2 metres. Another hybrid of similar stature is *D.* X *lemoinei*, which has white flowers. The cultivar 'Compacta' is much smaller, reaching 125 centimetres.

Perhaps the most popular are the many cultivars of *D. gracilis*. This species is quite small, generally less than 150 centimetres, but the cultivars are smaller again, at only 60 centimetres, making them useful for the edges of shrub borders or in a rock garden. 'Nikko' and Yuki Snowflake® have white flowers; Yuki Cherry Blossom® has pink. Grown for its radiant yellow summer foliage is Chardonnay Pearls®. 'Variegata' has white marbled foliage, while Crème Fraiche® has white-edged leaves. These last three all have white flowers. It should be noted that none of the above deutzia have appreciable

Deutzia X *hybrida* 'Strawberry Fields'.

Deutzia longifolia 'Veitchii'.

TODD BOLAND

Deutzia scabra 'Plena'.

fall colour and the flowering season is only about two weeks. They are not susceptible to insects or disease; however, they can be short-lived, especially *D. gracilis*. Propagation is by both summer and hardwood cuttings. They are hardy through zone 5, but *D. gracilis* can survive in zone 4 with adequate snow cover or if given extra winter protection.

Diervilla
BUSH HONEYSUCKLE

Bush honeysuckle, *Diervilla lonicera*, is native throughout Atlantic Canada. The genus name honours French surgeon Diere de Diereville, who introduced the plant to Europe around 1700. *Diervilla* has only recently been investigated as a potential garden ornamental. Multi-stemmed and suckering, *Diervilla* reaches about 1 metre. The lance-shaped to elliptical leaves emerge bronzy green, becoming glossy deep green, then turning a mix of yellow, orange, and red in autumn. In late spring to early summer they produce small clusters of yellow tubular flowers, which are appreciated by hummingbirds and butterflies. 'Copper' was selected for its exceptional coppery red spring foliage. Closely related is mountain bush-honeysuckle, *D. rivularis*, native to the eastern US. Its named selections include Summer Star™, with abundant yellow flowers; Kodiak® Black, purple summer foliage; Kodiak® Red, red spring and fall foliage; Kodiak® Orange, orange spring and fall foliage; and Honeybee®, bright yellow summer foliage. Also noteworthy is the hybrid Firefly Nightglow™, which has dark purple-black summer foliage that turns fiery red in autumn.

Bush honeysuckle, a tough, resilient plant, can tolerate poor, dry, rocky, acidic soil. Grow it in full sun or part shade. It may be naturalized as a ground cover on slopes or under tall trees. Few pests or diseases bother it, but occasionally powdery mildew can be problematic. Propagation is by summer cuttings or, more commonly, through removal of the suckers. Bush honeysuckle is hardy to zone 3; mountain bush honeysuckle, rated for zone 5.

Diervilla lonicera.

Eleutherococcus sieboldianus 'Variegatus'.

Eleutherococcus sieboldianus
FIVE-FINGER ARALIA

There are 38 species of *Eleutherococcus*, close relatives of Aralia. In Atlantic Canada, we only grow one species, the Chinese *E. sieboldianus*, commonly called the five-fingered aralia, a reference to its five-leaflet palmate leaves. It is a suckering, upright shrub up to 2 to 3 metres tall with spiny stems and 10-centimetre-wide bright green leaves. It retains its leaves well into the fall but has no appreciable fall colour. Plants are dioecious with small umbels of greenish white flowers in June. If pollinated, female plants produce clusters of black berries. While the plain green version is occasionally seen, more popular is the cultivar 'Variegatus', which has bright green leaflets elegantly edged in white. Five-fingered aralia is useful in naturalized settings or as a living screen/informal hedge. The variegated cultivar is useful as a foliage contrast in a mixed shrub border.

Five-fingered aralia are care-free, good for nearly any well-drained soil, in sun or shade. It is one of the best shrubs for dry shade. Few insects or diseases bother it. Propagation is by summer cuttings. It is rated hardy to zone 4.

TODD BOLAND

Euonymus
WINTERCREEPER, BURNING BUSH, SPINDLETREE

Of the 130 or more species of *Euonymus*, only three are usually grown in Atlantic Canada, two of which are very popular; the other, more uncommon. Burning bush, *E. alatus*, is native to northern China and Japan. It is perhaps the best deciduous shrub to grow for autumn foliage. Some plants are fiery red; others, cherry red. Either way, they colour up by late September, earlier than most deciduous shrubs. The species can reach 3 metres and has paired elliptical leaves and distinct corky ridges along their stems. Their yellow-green flowers are insignificant and become red fruit in autumn. Also popular is 'Compactus', which has smaller leaves and less ridged bark and forms a globe up to 2.5 metres tall and wide. 'Chicago Fire', also compact, is considered the hardiest of the burning bushes. For small gardens try Little Moses™, which tops at about 1 metre. Less commonly seen but still desirable is European spindletree, *E. europeaus*. It appears much like a small tree form of a burning bush, reaching 5 metres. It also has spectacular fall colour, with the bonus of decorative pinkish red fruit. Both species are grown as lawn specimens, less commonly as hedges or living screens.

Euonymus fortunei 'Canadale Gold'.

Euonymus alatus.

The other popular species is the broad-leaved evergreen wintercreeper, *E. fortunei*, a native of China and Japan. It is most commonly grown as a low, ground-cover-like shrub or clipped into mounds. However, if given the proper support, it can climb to 3 metres or more. This species has paired, rounded, leathery leaves and insignificant greenish yellow flowers. Many available cultivars are selected for their decoratively marked leaves. With white-edged leaves are 'Emerald Gaiety' and 'Silver Queen'. For yellow-edged leaves try 'Emerald'n'Gold' (pink highlights in winter), 'Canadale Gold', and Gold Splash®. With yellow-centred, green-edged leaves are 'Surespot', 'Moonshadow', and Blondie®. A few cultivars have plain green leaves: 'Kewensis' (white veins), 'Coloratus' (purplish in winter), and 'Sarcoxie' (plain green year-round).

Burning bush require full sun and evenly moist, fertile soil. Fall colour is poor if it is grown in too much shade. Wintercreeper takes full sun to full shade but needs evenly moist soil. Neither tolerate wet or dry soils. Leaf spot is sometimes an issue, but insects rarely are. Propagation is by summer cuttings or, in the case of burning bush, hardwood cuttings as well. Burning bush and European spindletree are hardy to zone 4; wintercreeper is better in zone 5 or milder. Strong winter sun and wind can burn their foliage even in zone 6.

Euonymus fortunei 'Silver Queen'.

Exochorda X *macrantha* 'The Bride'.

Exochorda X *macrantha*
PEARLBUSH

This small genus of flowering shrub is native to China and central Asia. The only one likely to be found in Atlantic Canada is *Exochorda* X *macrantha* 'The Bride'. This hybrid, which may reach 1.2 metres, has a mounding habit with arching branches. Its oblong, 5-centimetre-wide leaves are matte green in summer and yellow in autumn. In May-June, the stems are covered in masses of white, five-petalled flowers which are held in 7- to 10-centimetre-long clusters. It is an excellent shrub for a mixed border or massed along foundations.

Pearlbush do well in most well-drained soil; however, it performs best in reasonably fertile soil which is slightly acidic. Full sun produces the best floral display. It is surprisingly drought-tolerant. Few pests or diseases bother pearlbush. Propagation is by summer cuttings. It is hardy to zone 5.

Forsythia
FORSYTHIA

Forsythia is a harbinger of spring, blooming in April and May—before the plants produce leaves. There are a dozen species, most native to China, with one native to Europe. In the garden, Atlantic Canadian gardeners grow mostly *F.* X *intermedia*, a hybrid between *F. suspensa* and *F. viridissima*. The genus is named for William Forsyth (1737–1804), a Scottish botanist who was a royal head gardener and a founding member of the Royal Horticultural Society. Forsythia are broad-spreading shrubs typically between 2 to 3 metres tall. Leaves are elliptical to lance-shaped, waxy, and turn purple-red in autumn. Nearly stemless, yellow, 3-centimetre-wide bell-like flowers clothe the stems in mid-spring. The floral display can be outstanding. Not surprising, they are popular landscape shrubs as lawn specimens or in mixed shrub borders. They may also be used as living screens and informal hedging.

One of the oldest cultivars is 'Spectabilis', which can reach 2.5 metres. However, it is not as hardy as many of the newer cultivars. 'Northern Gold' (3 metres), 'Lynwood Gold' (2 me-

Forsythia 'Goldrush'.

Forsythia X *intermedia* 'Spectabilis'.

tres), 'Goldrush' (2 metres), Magical® Gold (2 metres), 'Kolgold' (1.7 metres), 'New Hampshire Gold' (1.5 metres), and 'Ottawa' (1.5 metres) are all similar to 'Spectabilis' but hardier. While the above are broad shrubs, the Show Off® series have a narrow, upright habit. Show Off® reaches 1.7 metres; Show Off Starlet®, 1 metre; and Show Off Sugar Baby®, a mere 75 centimetres. Gold Tide® is also low, at 80 centimetres, but has spreading, arching stems. 'Happy Centennial', at 1 metre, is perhaps the hardiest of the smaller selections. Forsythia are generally uninteresting in summer, but new variegated types, despite not having as significant a floral display, are charming all summer. 'Golden Times', at 1.5 metres, has yellow-edged leaves; Citrus Swizzle™, a dwarf 60-centimetre counterpart. 'Fiesta' has reverse yellow variegation and reaches 1 metre. 'Kumson' has appealing white-veined leaves and reaches 2 metres.

Forsythia are generally care-free plants. Any well-drained soil in full sun keeps them healthy. Propagation is by summer cuttings. The main pests are aphids or spider mites; the main disease, leaf spots. However, forsythia are primarily affected by winter cold. While many of the above cultivars are hardy to zone 4, they may lose their flowers if the temperature drops below -20°C. This is most obvious in areas with significant snowfall, where those branches below the snow flower regularly, while those above fail to bloom.

Forsythia X *intermedia* 'Northern Gold'.

Fothergilla
Dwarf fothergilla, witch alder

Only two species fall within the genus *Fothergilla*, *F. gardenii* and *F. major*, both natives of the southeastern US. The genus name honours English physician and botanist Dr. John Fothergill (1712–1780). *Fothergilla gardenii*, the smaller of the two, forms a mounding, suckering, deciduous shrub that remains less than 90 centimetres; *F. major* is larger, reaching 3 metres or more in height. Both have thick-textured, oval leaves that are ribbed, with distinct toothed edges along their outer half. The summer foliage is often tinted blue-green and typically develops brilliant fall colours in shades of red, orange, and yellow. Just before (*F. gardenii*) or shortly after (*F. major*) the leaves unfurl, plants produce fragrant, white, bottlebrush-like flowers up to 5 centimetres long. Selections of *F. gardenii* include 'Suzanne', which rarely exceeds 60 centimetres tall; 'Harold Epstein', at 40 centimetres; 'Blue Mist', which has distinct blue-tinted foliage; and

Fothergilla gardenii.

'Appalachia', which has exceptional fall colour. The most common selection of *F. major* is 'Arkansas Beauty', which is more compact than the species with glossier green foliage and has better drought tolerance. Hybrids between the two above species are also known. 'Mount Airy', the standard, is selected primarily for its easy rootability. It can reach 1.8 metres. 'Red Monarch'

Fothergilla gardenii 'Blue Shadow'.

Fothergilla 'Mount Airy'.
LEFT: *Fothergilla gardenii* 'Blue Mist'.

Genista
BROOM, DYER'S GREENWOOD

Most of the over 100 species of *Genista* are common around the Mediterranean. They vary tremendously in size but all have similar small, yellow, pealike flowers. They are closely related to the genus *Cytisus*, also known as brooms. Four species are prevalent in Atlantic Canada: *G. pilosa*, *G. sagittalis*, *G. lydia*, and *G. tinctoria*. Perhaps the most popular species is *G. pilosa* 'Vancouver Gold', also known as creeping broom. As the common name suggests, this species has a creeping, ground-cover-like habit with grey-green stems and small, deep green leaves. In June or July, the plants are covered in solitary yellow blossoms. 'Gold Flash' is similar. *Genista sagittalis*, called winged broom, also has a ground-cover-like habit, but its flattened, green stems can reach 30 centimetres. Its flowers are in terminal clusters. Both are ideal along pathways, retaining walls, and dry embankments or in a rock garden setting.

Dyer's greenwood, *G. tinctoria*, a rounded shrub to 90 centimetres, has green stems and small, almost insignificant, leaves. It has terminal ra-

and 'Red Licorice' were both selected for their reliable red fall colour. 'Sea Spray' has bluer foliage than the norm, while 'Blue Shadow', a mutation of 'Mount Airy', has outstanding powder blue foliage. 'Windy City' has plain green leaves but exceptional hardiness.

Fothergilla prefer evenly moist, acidic, organic-rich but well-drained soil in full sun; however, in hot locations afternoon shade will help them thrive. *Fothergilla major* tolerate some drought. These care-free shrubs are rarely bothered by pests or disease. With early flowers and spectacular fall colour, *Fothergilla* are wonderful shrubs to grow as specimens or accents in shrub borders, along foundations, or as an informal hedge. Plant them near the front of a border so that their unique fragrant flowers and attractive fall colour can be best appreciated. Propagation is by seed or summer cuttings. Both species are hardy to zone 5, with 'Windy City' hardy to zone 4.

Genista pilosa 'Vancouver Gold'.

Genista sagittalis.

cemes of golden yellow flowers in mid-late summer. *Genista lydia* reaches only 60 centimetres, with a domed habit and arching green stems. Both are useful along the front of dry shrub borders or large rockeries.

Genista like hot, sunny locations with well-drained soil. They perform a little better in poor soil than rich. They are very drought-tolerant. *Genista* are a little tougher than *Cytisus* and can be used in windier locations. Pests and diseases are rare, but winter wet can cause root rot. All attract bees. Propagation is by summer cuttings. The above are hardy to zone 4, except winged broom, which is rated for zone 5.

Genista tinctoria.

Hamamelis
WITCH-HAZEL

Of the six species of *Hamamelis*, four are from the Americas, one from China, and one from Japan. The genus name comes from the Greek words *hama*, at the same time, and *melon*, fruit, in reference to the plant having both fruit and flowers simultaneously. The flowers of all species are axillary, with four narrow straplike but often curled petals and four short but noticeable maroon-purple sepals. The flowers, often fragrant, come in shades of yellow, bronze, orange, red, or purple. The flowering season is either mid-late fall or late winter to early spring, depending on the species. The foliage is oval, ribbed, and sharply toothed. The fall colour ranges from yellow, orange, or red and can often be quite striking.

The most popular American species are *H. vernalis* and *H. virginiana*. The former has late-winter or early spring flowers in the variety of colours noted above; the later produces yellow flowers

Hamamelis X *intermedia* 'Jelena'.

Hamamelis X *intermedia* 'Ruby Glow'.

in fall just as the leaves drop. Both grow up to 2 to 3 metres and generally have yellow fall colour. They are native to the mountainous areas of the eastern US. Named selections of *H. vernalis* include 'Sandra' (yellow), 'Quasimodo' (orange), 'Amethyst' (purplish pink), and 'Autumn Embers' (yellow with multicoloured fall foliage).

More popular is the hybrid *H.* X *intermedia*, created from the two Asian species *H. mollis* and *H. japonica*. It is typically larger than the American species, reaching 3 to 5 metres. Its flowers are a little larger than the American species and it blooms mid-winter to early spring. Its fall colour is generally more desirable than that of the American counterparts. The most easily found named selections are 'Sunburst' (pale yellow), 'Primavera' (light yellow), 'Arnold's Promise' (bright yellow), 'Barmstedt Gold' (golden yellow), 'Jelena' (orange), 'Feuerzauber' (orange-red), 'Diane' (orange-red), and 'Ruby Glow' (red).

Witch-hazel prefer acidic, well-drained, humus-rich soil in sun or part shade. Too dry soil can lead to leaf scorch. Witch-hazel are commonly grown naturalized under taller deciduous trees or along the edges of woodlands. As many of the *H.* X *intermedia* hybrids are grafted, promptly remove any suckers that form. Pests and diseases are generally not a problem but witch-hazel are occasionally bothered by Japanese beetles, leafrollers, and, if grown in too sheltered a site, powdery mildew. Propagation is by grafting or, in the case of the species, by seed. *Hamamelis virginiana* is the hardiest, rated for zone 3; *H. vernalis*, zone 4; and *H.* X *intermedia*, zone 5.

Hamamelis X *intermedia* 'Arnold's Promise'.

TODD BOLAND

Heptacodium miconoides.

Heptacodium miconoides
SEVEN-SON FLOWER

Seven-son flower, *Heptacodium miconoides*, a deciduous shrub native to China, has an irregular shape, reaching 4 to 5 metres tall, although often less than 3 metres in Atlantic Canada. The shiny narrow leaves do not have appreciable fall colour. Seven-son flower is valued for its late-season blooms; rounded clusters of fragrant white flowers in September are followed by reddish pink fruit in late fall. Butterflies visit their late flowers. The exfoliating, shredded bark adds winter interest to the landscape.

Seven-son flower need full sun and a sheltered, warm site. It performs best in warmer areas of Nova Scotia and, while hardy in eastern Newfoundland, rarely manages to bloom before it is cut down by frost. Pests and diseases are not a problem. Propagation is by seed or summer cuttings. It is rated hardy to zone 5.

Hibiscus syriacus
ROSE-OF-SHARON

Rose-of-Sharon, a native of China, is second to none for its glorious display of late-season flowers. The wild form can reach 4 metres in height and has 7-centimetre-wide pink flowers with red eyes from midsummer to mid-fall. Each flower lasts only a day or two. The glossy deciduous leaves are three-lobed and coarsely toothed but have no appreciable fall colour. Popular cultivars include 'Minerva' (lavender-pink), 'Blue Bird' (lavender-blue), 'Mathilde' (pink), 'Aphrodite' (pink), 'Helene' (white, red eye), and 'Diana' (pure white). Double-flowered selections include 'Collie Mullen' (pink), 'Lucy' (deep pink), 'Blushing Bride' (pale pink), and the Chiffon™ series in blue, lavender, pink, and white. If space is at a premium, try one of the Lil' Kim® series, which top at 1.2 metres tall.

Rose-of-Sharon are easily grown in most soil types but does not tolerate wet soil. Full sun is best for maximum flower production. It is often grown as a stand-alone specimen or along foundations and among mixed shrub borders. It is also used for hedging or as a screen. Propaga-

Hibiscus syriacus 'Pink Chiffon'.

Hibiscus syriacus 'Minerva'.

Hippophae rhamnoides.

tion is by summer cuttings. The main diseases are various fungal leaf spotting, rust, or canker. Aphids may sometimes be problematic, but the most serious pest is Japanese beetles, which can defoliate the plant. While hardy to zone 5, rose-of-Sharon, a heat lover, requires a sunny hot spot for peak performance. Due to a lack of summer heat, it is a challenging shrub to grow in Newfoundland.

Hippophae rhamnoides
Sea buckthorn

It is with some reservation that sea buckthorn, *Hippophae rhamnoides*, is included here—its suckering habit can make it invasive when conditions allow. However, it is one of the few silvery landscape shrubs we can grow in Atlantic Canada. Sea buckthorn, a large shrub, reaches 3 to 4 metres in height. It has spiny stems and narrow, lance-shaped, silvery green leaves up to 7 centimetres long. They have no significant fall colour. Plants are dioecious, with separate male and female plants. In spring, insignificant but fragrant yellow-green flowers appear, which, on female plants, become orange berries which can last well into the winter. This fruit is edible and high in Vitamins A, C, and E. To obtain fruit, you must plant both male and female shrubs near each other. This plant is useful as a windbreak or living screen.

Sea buckthorn are sun-lovers and require well-drained soil; winter wet can cause root rot. It is drought- and wind-tolerant and, as the common name suggests, also salt-tolerant, making it a useful shrub for seaside gardens. It can also grow well on poor, gravelly sites. Propagation is by summer cuttings or through sucker removal. Sea buckthorn is overall a care-free, super hardy plant, zone 3, so it may be cultivated throughout Atlantic Canada.

Hydrangea
Hydrangea

Of the 70 species of Hydrangea, only five are commonly grown in Atlantic Canada as garden ornamentals—*H. macrophylla*, *H. paniculata*, *H. arborescens*, *H. quercifolia*, and *H. anomala* ssp. *petiolaris*. The first three are extremely popular, with new cultivars being released each year. The last one, a vine, is described in the vines section. All have a combination of small fertile flowers and larger sterile flowers among their inflorescence.

From Asia comes *Hydrangea macrophylla*, the

Hydrangea arborescens 'Invincibelle® Spirit'.
PREVIOUS SPREAD: *Hydrangea arborescens* 'Annabelle' and *H. macrophylla* 'Nikko Blue'.

popular mophead and lacecap hydrangea. The mopheads typically have a large rounded head of mostly sterile flowers; the lacecaps are flat-topped with small fertile inner flowers surrounded by larger sterile outer flowers. In the wild, this species can reach 3 metres, but most modern cultivars are 1.5 to 2 metres. The flower colours of these hydrangea are affected by variations in soil pH. Most gardeners prefer a rich blue colour, which is achieved under acidic soil conditions. With nearly neutral soil pH, the flowers are purple; under alkaline conditions, they are pink. 'Nikko Blue', one of the oldest cultivars, is still widely available. Perhaps the most popular is the Endless Summer® series, which have repeat blooms from late summer through fall. For smaller gardens, the dwarf Cityline® and Seaside Serenade® series are ideal, as most top at about 1 metre in height. The Abracadabra® and Onyx® series have typical mophead blooms but contrasting black stems. Everlasting® Revolution is unique in having flowers which may be pink, purple, or blue on the same plant. Among the lacecaps, the older standard cultivars are 'Blue Wave' and 'Blue Bird'; newer selections such as Twist-n-Shout® are more compact, with repeat blooms. For double flowers, try the Double Delights™ series, whose sterile flowers are double. For variegated leaves, look for 'Lemon Wave', with yellow-edged leaves, and 'Variegata' and Light-O-Day®, with white-edged leaves.

The panicle or PG hydrangea, *H. paniculata*, also from Asia, is the largest of the shrubby garden hydrangea, reaching 8 metres tall, although most modern-day cultivars are less than 3 metres. They have large cone-shaped flower heads that generally start green, turn white, and then turn pink as they age. The blooming season runs from August to severe frost. 'Grandiflora', the oldest and tallest cultivar with nearly all sterile flowers, is often trained to a single stem to create a tree form. Newer cultivars, reaching 2 to 3 metres, are 'Phantom', 'The Swan', and Strawberry Vanilla®. Similar but smaller selections, nearly 1.5 metres tall, are 'Polar Bear', Sweet Summer®, 'Silver Dollar', and White Diamonds®. Magical® Moonlight has double sterile flowers. If space is a consideration, try one of the dwarf cultivars: 'Little Lamb', Little

Hydrangea quercifolia 'Little Honey'.

Quick Fire®, Bobo®, Baby Lace®, or Diamond Rouge®. Several recent cultivars have flowers that turn nearly red as they age, including 'Pink Diamond', Fire Light®, Quick Fire®, Pinky Winky®, Magical Fire®, and Zinfin Doll®. For something different, try one of the green-flowered cultivars, such as 'Limelight', which reaches nearly 3 metres tall, or Little Lime®, which is half the height.

Smooth hydrangea, *H. arborescens*, is unique among the popular garden hydrangeas: as it blooms on new wood, it can be hard-pruned each year. Native to the eastern US, the wild form produces large rounded heads of white flowers nearly 20 to 25 centimetres wide. It can reach 1.5 metres tall and blooms from midsummer into autumn. Flowers may turn light pink or green as they age. 'Annabelle', the oldest selection, is still popular. Incrediball® has magnificent flower heads that sometimes surpass 30 centimetres in diameter. Incrediball® Blush has pink-tinted flowers. Invincibelle® Spirit has smaller flower heads, around 15 centimetres wide, which are pink when they open; Invincibelle® Ruby flowers are deep reddish pink. Unique is White Dome®, whose domed flower heads consist of mostly fertile flowers with just a ring of larger sterile flowers; this imparts a lacy effect. 'Hayes Starburst' is similar, but the sterile flowers are double.

From southeastern US comes oak-leaf hydrangea, *H. quercifolia*, whose leaves are nearly as ornamental as the flowers. As the common name suggests, its oak-shaped leaves are lobed and coarsely serrated. The fall foliage is the most striking of any hydrangea, turning from orange to red to burgundy. Its white flowers, a combination of fertile and sterile, are held in conelike clusters similar to those of PG hydrangea. Most selections reach 1.8 to 2.5 metres. 'Snow Queen' is a tall white-flowered selection, while 'Pee Wee'

Hydrangea paniculata 'Limelight'.

and 'Munchkin' are dwarf versions at 1.2 metres and 1 metre respectively. 'Snowflake' is grown for its double sterile flowers. 'Amethyst' is a taller selection whose flowers age from light pink to dark reddish pink; 'Ruby Slippers' is a similar but compact 1.2-metre selection. 'Little Honey' is a dwarf 1.2-metre selection grown primarily for its charming golden yellow to chartreuse leaves.

In general, hydrangea prefer well-drained organic-rich soil. They do not tolerate drought. While acidic soil is needed to keep the mopheads and lacecaps blue, pH does not affect the colours of the other types. Full sun is best for PG hydrangea, but the others grow well under part shade. Oakleaf hydrangea tolerate the most shade. Hydrangea are popular as foundation plants or even mixed in flower borders. Propagation is by summer cuttings. For the most part, few pests or diseases bother them, but powdery mildew is occasional if they are grown in sheltered sites. PG and smooth hydrangea are hardy to zone 3, and, while rated hardy to zone 5, the oakleaf, lacecaps, and mopheads are more reliable bloomers in zone 6. As a rule, mophead and oakleaf hydrangea need a very sheltered site in Newfoundland; while they often grow well, they tend not to produce many flowers.

Hypericum
ST. JOHN'S-WORT

Most *Hypericum* are herbaceous plants; quite a few are weedy in nature. A limited number of shrubby species can be grown locally. *Hypericum calycinum* is technically a broad-leaved evergreen but can be semi-deciduous or dieback to the ground in Atlantic Canada. Plants reach 30 to 45 centimetres, with paired, ovate, waxy leaves. From midsummer into fall, they produce solitary, 5-centimetre-diameter yellow flowers with pincushion-like stamens. 'Hidcote' is a similar hybrid with even larger flowers, up to 7 centimetres in diameter, on plants up to 90 centimetres tall. Other similar species include *H. frondosum*, *H. forrestii*, *H. henryi*, and *H. kouytchense*. *Hypericum kalmianum* is also evergreen to semi-deciduous, reaching 90 centimetres but has smaller, 4-centimetre-wide flowers in clusters. The above *Hypericum* are useful for foundation plantings and naturalized settings or near the front of a mixed shrub border.

Hypericum forrestii.

Hypericum 'Hidcote'.

Hypericum prefer full sun and fertile, well-drained soil. Because they dislike windy locations, select a warm, sheltered site. To retain some leaves, winter protection is suggested; however, if dieback is severe in winter, plants may be hard-pruned and still provide flowers, as they bloom on new wood. Pests and diseases are uncommon. Propagation is by summer cuttings or, for species, by seed. The hardiest species is *H. kalmianum*, zone 4. *Hypericum calycinum* and 'Hidcote' are hardy for zone 5, while the rest, rated hardy to zone 6, are only useful in the mildest areas of Atlantic Canada.

Ilex
HOLLY

Over 400 species of holly are found throughout the world, from sub-arctic to tropical regions. While a few have widespread distributions, many are rare and endangered endemics. Most are broad-leaved evergreens, but several of the northern species are deciduous. Size varies tremendously from low creeping shrubs to trees up to 30 metres tall. Some have spiny-tipped foliage, while others have smooth-edged leaves. All are dioecious, with separate male and female plants. The flowers are generally white and not particularly showy. If pollinated, female plants develop decorative berries (botanically drupes) that often remain on the plant for several months, particularly over the winter. In temperate climates, the winter berries are often the main attraction for the plant, if robins and waxwings have not eaten them.

From an ornamental perspective, the most important species is the English holly, *I. aquifolium*. It is a broad-leaved evergreen shrub that is commonly between 2 and 4 metres tall, but may infrequently reach 10 metres. It has been grown for hundreds of years and, today, there are numerous cultivars, many of which have white or yellow variegated, stiff, spiny-tipped leaves. The more popular white-edged cultivars include 'Argentea Marginata' (female), 'Ferox Argentea' (super-spiny foliaged male), 'Silver Queen', and 'Silver King'. Among the yellow-edged cultivars are 'Aurea Marginata' (female) and 'Madame Briot' (female). 'Amber' and 'Bacciflava' are green-leaved females that produce yellow fruit. 'Hibernica' has green leaves that lack the spiny lobes. 'Angustifolia' is a male with very narrow spiny-tipped leaves and narrow pyramidal habit. 'Alaska', a spiny green-leaved female cultivar, is hardier than most English holly. As English holly is not particularly hardy, it requires a sheltered location. The green-leaved cultivars are hardier than the variegated.

Far more popular in Atlantic Canada is blue holly, *Ilex* X *meservae*. This is a hybrid between English holly and a hardy Chinese species called *I. rugosa*. The hybrids generally have a broad, bushy habit with foliage more akin to that of

Ilex X *meservae* 'Blue Princess'.

Ilex verticillata.

English holly. Most are very dark green with attractive glossy foliage. Popular male-female combinations include 'Blue Boy' and 'Blue Girl', 'Blue Prince and Blue Princess', China Boy® and China Girl®, and Blue Maid® and Blue Stallion®. Other cultivars include Blue Angel®, 'Golden Girl' (yellow fruit), Castle Wall® (male columnar), and 'Centennial Girl' (female columnar). A female cultivar, 'Honey Maid' is notable for its grey-green leaves edged in white.

Box-leaved holly, *I. crenata*, is different from the previous species. It is evergreen but its leaves are rounded and lack spiny tips. It forms a rounded bush 1.5 to 3 metres tall. The females have black fruit. Popular cultivars include 'Sky Pencil' (columnar female, 3 metres in height), 'Jersey Pinnacle' (pyramidal male, 2.5 metres), Sky Pointer™ (narrow pyramidal male, 150 centimetres), 'Convexa' (rounded male, 2 metres), 'Helleri' (dwarf rounded female, 1.2 metres), 'Hetzii' (similar to 'Helleri'), 'Dwarf Pagoda' (dwarf male, 60 to 100 centimetres), 'Green Dragon' (very dwarf male, 45 centimetres), and 'Drops of Gold' (a yellow-leaved mutation of 'Hetzii').

Native to eastern North America, including Nova Scotia, is inkberry, *I. glabra*, a rounded, suckering evergreen bush 1.5 to 2.5 metres tall. It has smooth-edged, spoon-shaped leaves and black fruit on females. 'Shamrock', 'Densa', Nordic®, and Green Gem® are compact cultivars reaching about 60 to 90 centimetres.

Winterberry holly, *I. verticillata*, which reaches 3 metres tall, is a deciduous species native throughout Atlantic Canada. It is often found along streams and pond margins. It is grown for its orange berries, which remain on the naked stems all winter. Cultivars are available with yellow, orange, or red fruit. The Berry Heavy® series 'Winter Gold' and 'Winter Red' are recommended. If space is limited, try Berry Poppins® and Mr. Poppins®, both dwarf selections topping at 1.2 metres. Also native throughout Atlantic Canada is mountain holly, *I. mucronata* (formerly known as *Nemopanthus mucronata*): this deciduous species can reach 2 to 5 metres tall and has yellow fall foliage; the females have long-stemmed matte red fruit.

The above holly all prefer humus-rich, evenly moist, acidic soil. Inkberry, winterberry, and mountain holly tolerate quite wet sites. Full sun is best but part shade is tolerated. Propagation is by summer or fall cuttings. Few pests or diseases bother holly. Both male and female plants must be grown near each other to obtain fruit. Blue holly and English holly pollinate each other. Mountain holly is hardy to zone 2; winterberry holly, zone 3; and inkberry and blue holly, zone 4. As English holly and box-leaved holly are only reliably hardy to zone 6, they are useful only in the mildest areas of Nova Scotia and southeastern Newfoundland. The variegated forms of English holly are only suited to southernmost Nova Scotia.

Itea virginica.

Itea virginica.

Itea virginica
Sweetspire

Most of the 10 species of *Itea* are broad-leaved evergreens from China—but a single deciduous species comes from eastern North America: Virginia sweetspire, *I. virginica*. This plant, which can reach 1 to 2 metres tall, has a loose, suckering habit with arching stems. The shiny leaves are lance-shaped and turn a mix of yellow, orange, and burgundy-red in the fall. In early summer to midsummer, plants produce narrow, 5- to 10-centimetre-long bottlebrush-like, fragrant white flowers. 'Henry's Garnet' is a compact 1-metre cultivar with outstanding burgundy fall colour and flower sprays up to 15 centimetres long. 'Little Henry' is even more compact, often reaching just 70 centimetres. Sweetspire is most often used as a foundation plant, along the edges of woodlands or in wet depressions.

Virginia sweetspire grow in full sun or full shade; however, the best fall colour and heaviest flower production occur in brighter light conditions. The soil should be acidic, humus-rich, and evenly moist; however, it adapts to a variety of soil types. Propagation is by sucker division or by summer cuttings. It has no known serious pest or disease issues. Hardy to zone 5, it needs some summer heat to do well and performs best in southern Nova Scotia.

Kerria japonica
JAPANESE KERRIA

Kerria japonica, the only species within the genus *Kerria*, is a native of China, Korea, and Japan. The genus name honours William Kerr, a gardener in Kew in the early 1800s. Japanese kerria is a wide-spreading, suckering shrub with arching stems, reaching 2 to 3 metres tall. The leaves are lance-shaped and coarsely toothed, bright green in summer and yellow in fall. The stems are green all season, lending this shrub winter interest. The 3- to 5-centimetre-wide flowers, produced in May or June, are yellow with five petals. While the single-flowered cultivar 'Golden Guinea' is occasionally seen, far more popular is the double form 'Pleniflora', whose flowers look like yellow pompoms. For something different, try 'Picta', a dwarf 70-centimetre-tall shrub which has single flowers but alluring grey-green leaves edged in white. Japanese kerria is useful in mixed shrub borders, along foundations, or in naturalized settings. It may even be used as an informal hedge.

Kerria japonica 'Pleniflora'.

Japanese kerria grow well in most soils and, once established, are reasonably drought-tolerant. This flowering shrub does best in part shade, as full sun can bleach its flowers. It tolerates full shade, but at the expense of good flowering. Pests are rare but leaf spotting, blights, and root rot are known. Propagation is by summer cuttings. It is hardy to zone 4.

Kolkwitzia amabilis
BEAUTYBUSH

Beautybush, a native of China, can reach more than 2.75 metres tall. It forms a dense, twiggy shrub with arching stems. The Latin name honours Richard Kolkwitz, a German botanist at the turn of the 20th century. In June or July, the plant is covered in light pink, yellow-throated flowers. Blossoms are trumpetlike and produced in small clusters. The dark green foliage, which turns yellow in autumn, is oval in outline and

Kerria japonica 'Picta'.

RIGHT: *Kolkwitzia amabilis* 'Pink Cloud'.

up to 10 centimetres long. The exfoliating bark provides winter interest. 'Pink Cloud' is the most popular cultivar but perhaps showier is Dream Catcher™, which has gold and orange summer foliage, a pleasant contrast to the pink flowers. Beautybush may be grown as a stand-alone shrub but is more commonly in mixed shrub borders or as an informal hedge.

Beautybush, care-free plants with few insect or disease concerns, prefer full sun but tolerate some shade. It will thrive in just about any well-drained soil. Propagation is by summer cuttings. It is rated hardy to zone 4.

Lavendula angustifolia
LAVENDER

While lavender is often used in perennial borders, it is, in fact, a dwarf shrub. In Atlantic Canada, only English lavender, *Lavendula angustifolia*, is reliably hardy. Lavender typically grows 30 to 45 centimetres tall. The narrow, evergreen, grey-green leaves are highly fragrant but it is the dried flowers that are typically harvested for potpourri and sachets. These small purple flowers are produced at the ends of elongate stalks from July into August. Lavender was traditionally grown in herb gardens but is also an ideal plant for cottage gardens or rockeries. It may also be used as a low, formal hedge. The many named cultivars differ in height or in the shade of purple blue of the flowers. Popular cultivars include 'Hidcote', 'Munstead', 'Vera', 'Folgate', and 'Royal Velvet'.

Lavender, heat and sun lovers, prefer well-drained, sandy, alkaline soil. It is very drought-tolerant. Root rot is common in too fertile or heavy soil. Cold winter winds may kill these plants. Otherwise, few pests or diseases bother it. Propagation is by seed or summer cuttings. It is rated hardy to zone 5.

Lavendula angustifolia 'Munstead'.

Ligustrum vulgare.

Ligustrum
PRIVET

Privet, perhaps the overall best hedging shrub in Atlantic Canada, reach 5 metres but can be trimmed as low as 90 centimetres. The genus *Ligustrum* has about 50 species found across Eurasia. For hedging, *Ligustrum vulgare*, *L. amurense*, *L. obtusifolium*, and *L. ovalifolium* are a few of the species suitable for Atlantic Canada. Perhaps the most popular is 'Cheyenne', a selection of *L. vulgare*. These all have paired, elliptical, waxy green leaves. While they have no appreciable fall colour, they hold their leaves well into December. In June-July, they have 7- to 10-centimetre-long panicles of fragrant white flowers that become black fruit that remain on the shrub through most of the winter. However, if used for formal hedging, they rarely blossom. With more decorative foliage is the hybrid 'Vicaryi', whose leaves are golden in full sun or chartreuse in shade, or *L. ovalifolium* 'Aureum', whose variegated leaves are broadly margined in yellow.

Privet perform best in full sun with well-drained, reasonably fertile soil. It tolerates drought and salt. It can also tolerate shade, but if used as a formal hedge, it may appear thin. The most common insect pests are leaf miners, aphids, and Japanese beetles; among diseases, twig blight, leaf spots, and powdery mildew have been known to occur. Propagation is by summer or hardwood cuttings. Most are hardy to zone 4. 'Cheyenne' is considered the hardiest. 'Vicaryi' and *L. ovalifolium* 'Aureum' are tenderer, at zone 5.

Lonicera
HONEYSUCKLE

Honeysuckle fall into two main groups: shrubs and vines. Among the shrubby types, three main species are grown in Atlantic Canada. The most popular is Tatarian honeysuckle, *L. tatarica*. This Russian species can reach 2 to 4 metres. It has paired oval leaves that often have a blue tint. The fall foliage is not particularly attractive. In June, it produces paired, reddish pink flowers from the upper leaf axils. These develop into paired red fruit. 'Rosea' has bright pink blossoms; 'Zabelii', deep pink; and 'Arnold Red', dark cherry red flowers. Also from Russia is Amur honeysuckle,

Lonicera tatarica 'Rosea'.

Lonicera maackii.

L. maackii, which grows to 5 metres tall and has dark green foliage. It, too, has no appreciable fall colour. Its flowers are white, aging to golden yellow. Both species are coarse and can seed about. They may be used in naturalized settings or as living screens. Bees, butterflies, and hummingbirds visit their blossoms. Fly honeysuckle, *L. xylosteum*, ranges from Europe to Siberia. It can reach 3 metres tall and, like Tatarian honeysuckle, often has blue-tinted leaves. Its flowers are pale yellow. 'Emerald Mound', the only cultivar on the market, forms a dense globe up to 1 metre in diameter, making it popular for foundation plantings or more formal settings.

Challenging to find but well worth it is *L. fragrantissima*, commonly called winter honeysuckle or the sweet breath of spring. This Chinese shrub can reach 3 metres and has waxy rounded leaves with pale undersides. Its fall colour is yellow. In spring, before they leaf, it produces small clusters of lemon-scented white flowers.

Privet honeysuckle, *L. pileata*, is semi-evergreen with a trailing habit and small ovate glossy leaves. It is suitable as a ground cover. The flowers are insignificant. 'Variegata', which is more popular than the species, has yellow-edged foliage.

Shrub honeysuckle may be grown in sun or part shade and tolerates any conditions except wet sites. Tatarian, Amur, and fly honeysuckle are drought- and salt-tolerant and popular for seaside gardens. The main insect pests are moth larvae and the only serious disease is powdery mildew. Propagation is by seed, summer cuttings, or hardwood cuttings. The European and Russian species noted above are all hardy to zone 3; winter honeysuckle, zone 4; and privet honeysuckle, zone 6.

Magnolia stellata
Star magnolia

Most magnolia are trees, but the star magnolia, *M. stellata*, can be either tree or shrub. Sometimes it is more treelike, reaching 6 metres, while often, in Atlantic Canada, it forms rounded shrubs 3 to 4 metres tall. This Japanese species is one of the earliest magnolia to flower, in late April through May, blooming just before the leaves unfurl. Its white or pale pink spectacular flowers are soli-

Magnolia stellata 'Pink Star'.

SHRUBS AND VINES FOR ATLANTIC CANADA

Magnolia stellata 'Royal Star'.

Mahonia aquifolium.

tary, 10 centimetres in diameter, and highly fragrant. These open from pussywillow-like flower buds that remain on the shrub all winter, providing winter interest. Summer leaves are relatively large and elliptical but have no appreciable fall colour. 'Royal Star' is the most popular white-flowered selection. 'Waterlily' is similar but blooms about two weeks later. 'Rosea' and Centennial Blush™ have pale pink flowers.

Star magnolia prefer full sun and organic-rich, acidic soil. It makes an admirable companion for ericaceous shrubs like rhododendrons and mountain laurels. It does not tolerate drought, wetness, or salt. The flowers are easily damaged by wind and late frosts. Diseases and pests are almost unknown. Propagation is by seed or summer cuttings. It is rated hardy to zone 4.

Mahonia
Oregon-grape, Grape-holly

The 70 species of *Mahonia* are native to Central and North America and eastern Asia and the Himalayas. They are closely related to barberry, *Berberis*, and are now included in that genus, but as they are so well known by their old name, they will be described separately. As a group *Mahonia* are suckering broad-leaved evergreen shrubs with spiny-tipped, compound leaves and terminal racemes of small, often yellow, flowers which later develop into blue or black fruit. There are only a few commonly grown ornamental species. Perhaps the most popular is Oregon-grape, *M. aquifolium*. This western North American species, native from British Columbia to northern California, can reach 1 to 2 metres in height. New foliage is often red-tinted and turns glossy deep green. Mildly fragrant yellow flowers are produced in May, becoming blue berries by autumn. More widespread in the Rockies of western North America, the creeping Oregon-grape, *M. repens*, is a short (30-centimetre) version of Oregon-grape, but the flower clusters are more compact and the leaves are dull green.

Mahonia prefer acidic, humus-rich, evenly moist soil in full to part shade. Full sun can lead to leaf scorching, especially in winter. They also prefer a sheltered site, as they are prone to winter burn if exposed to winter winds. Unless you plan on naturalizing plants, excessive suckers should be removed to keep plants in bounds. All *Mahonia* fruit best if two or more plants are grown together. There are no serious pests or diseases. Propagation is by fall cuttings. The hardiest species is creeping Oregon-grape, which is hardy to zone 4; Oregon-grape, to zone 5.

Morella pensylvanica
Northern Bayberry

Northern bayberry is native to eastern North America, including Atlantic Canada. It was once classified as *Myrica pensylvanica* and is still known by that name in much of the literature. It is a dense mounding shrub that varies from 1 to 3 metres in height. The leaves are spoon-shaped, leathery, glossy, and fragrant when bruised. Northern bayberry keep their leaves late into the fall but have no appreciable fall colour. Plants are dioecious with insignificant flowers, but female plants develop stemless grey-blue berries in autumn, which remain on the plant all winter, providing winter interest. The wax from the berries is the source of bayberry fragrance in candles. It is not a commonly grown ornamental shrub, but its tolerance to wind and salt makes it useful for seaside gardens and roadsides. Silver Sprite™, a compact selection, rarely exceeds 1.5 metres; Bobbee™, also compact, has larger, wavy-edged foliage.

Morella pensylvanica.

Bayberry prefer acidic sandy-peaty soil that is evenly moist; adaptable, it tolerates wet to dry soil, infertile soil, and, as noted, wind and salt. Plant at least one male to pollinate the females. Full sun is best, but it tolerates part shade. Propagation is by seed or summer cuttings. It is overall a care-free plant. It is rated hardy to zone 4.

Morella pensylvanica.

Pachysandra terminalis.

Pachysandra
SPURGE

Of the five species of *Pachysandra*, four are from eastern Asia and one from eastern North America. The genus name comes from the Greek words *pachys*, thick, and *andros*, stamen, referring to the thick white filaments of the blossoms. All are suckering broad-leaved evergreen subshrubs which reach 30 centimetres. Their leaves are oval to spoon-shaped and often crowded toward the ends of the stems. The flowers, produced in May, are small, white, and bottlebrush-like. What the flowers lack in ornamental value, they make up for in being highly fragrant. Japanese spurge, *P. terminalis*, has highly glossy foliage and terminal flower spikes; *P. axillaris* looks similar but its flowers arise from the upper leaf axils. The North American Allegheny spurge, *P. procumbens*, has scalloped-edged leaves that are mottled brown and silver when they emerge but later become plain green. *P. terminalis* 'Silver Edge' has attractive variegated foliage. All of the above are commonly grown as ground covers in shady to partly shaded locations.

Pachysandra prefer humus-rich, evenly moist but well-drained soil. The Chinese species require acidic soil, while the Allegheny spurge grows in acidic or alkaline soil. Both *P. terminalis* and *P. procumbens* can tolerate some drought once they are established. All prefer part to full shade; leaves may burn in full sun, especially in winter. Propagation is by division of the suckers. While generally care-free, they can be susceptible to leaf blight. *Pachysandra procumbens* is rated for zone 4; *P. terminalis*, zone 5; and *P. axillaris*, zone 6.

Pachystima canbyi
CLIFF GREEN

Cliff green, *Pachystima canbyi*, a native of the Rocky Mountains, is a broad-leaved evergreen ground cover reaching 15 to 30 centimetres tall.

Pachysandra terminalis 'Silver Edge'.

NEXT PAGE: *Pachystima myrsinites.*

TODD BOLAND

The narrow leaves are glossy green in summer, becoming bronzed in winter. Tiny axillary green flowers are produced in June. Oregon boxwood, *P. myrsinites* (*P. myrtifolia*), is similar but reaches 100 centimetres, has pinkish flowers and has elliptical leaves with toothed edges. Both are useful as ground covers, especially in shade, as well as in woodland gardens and rockeries.

Cliff green grow in full sun to full shade. As it prefers well-drained alkaline soil, in most of Atlantic Canada a yearly dusting of lime is suggested. Few pests or diseases bother them. Propagation is by summer cuttings or plant division. Cliff green is hardy to zone 3; Oregon boxwood is tenderer, zone 5.

Paeonia suffruticosa
TREE PEONY

We generally think of peonies as herbaceous garden perennials but tree peonies are becoming more popular and are being offered by more nurseries. From a distance, they look like classic garden peonies but they have thick, aboveground stems from which the flowering branches develop. In ideal locations, tree peonies may reach 2 metres but generally they are 1 to 1.5 metres tall. Tree peony species include *Paeonia rockii*, *P. suffruticosa*, *P. delavayi*, and *P. ludlowii* but most offered today are hybrids, collectively called *Paeonia suffruticosa* or *P.* X *lemoinei*. Over 600 hybrids are currently available, from single flowered to fully double, from white through shades of pink, red, and yellow. They bloom in June and July. These plants are often expensive but very long-lived. They are more commonly grown in herbaceous flower borders than among other shrubs.

Tree peony need full sun and deep, rich, fertile soil. Place them in a sheltered site to protect their large blossoms. Unlike herbaceous peony, few pests or diseases bother the tree types. Propagation is by division for the hybrids or seeds for the species. They are hardy to zone 5, but, with proper winter protection, are known to survive in zone 4.

Paeonia rockii.

Paeonia delavayi hybrid.

Philadelphus
MOCK-ORANGE

About 60 species of *Philadelphus* are native across the northern hemisphere, with most found in China. All are grown for their white, fragrant flowers. The most popular species in Atlantic Canada is *P. coronarius*, a European native which has been growing in local gardens for over 100 years. This large deciduous shrub can reach 4 metres tall and has paired, ovate leaves and clusters of four-petalled 2.5- to 3.5-centimetre-diameter creamy white flowers in July. The leaves have no appreciable fall colour. The more popular hybrids have semi-double or double flowers and include 'Minnesota Snowflake' and 'Virginal'. Native to western North America is *P. lewisii*, a smaller 1.5- to 2-metre-tall shrub with snow-white flowers in June or early July. Popular cultivars include 'Blizzard', 'Cheyenne', and 'Goose Creek', the latter with double flowers. *P.* X *lemoinei* is another smaller hybrid reaching a height of 1.5 metres. 'Avalanche', often available, is the most fragrant mock-orange on the market, but perhaps the more attractive cultivar is 'Belle Etoile', whose white flowers have purple-red

Philadelphus coronarius.

Philadelphus coronarius 'Aureus'.

petal bases. With attractive summer foliage is *P. coronarius* 'Aureus', with bright yellow leaves, and Icelandic™, with variegated leaves. Both of these reach 2 metres. Consider 'Starbright', a hybrid released from the Memorial University Botanical Garden in St. John's, Newfoundland; it can reach 3 metres but the spring leaves are purple-tinted and its white flowers open from dark purple buds.

Mock-orange prefer full sun and well-drained but organic-rich soil. As most species originate from limestone regions, a yearly dusting of lime is beneficial. They tolerate some drought, but poorly drained soil can lead to root rot. Overall, pests and diseases are uncommon. Propagation is by either summer or hardwood cuttings. Most of the above mock-orange are hardy to zone 4. The *P. lewisii* cultivars may even survive zone 3, but the *P.* X *lemoinei* hybrids are only reliably hardy to zone 6.

Physocarpus opulifolius
NINEBARK

The genus name *Physocarpus* comes from the Greek *physa*, a bladder, and *karpos*, fruit, referring to the inflated dry fruits this plant produces. Of the 10 species of *Physocarpus*, Atlantic Canadian gardeners primarily grow *P. opulifolius*, a species native to eastern North America, as ornamentals. The wild species can reach 3 metres tall and has bright green, maplelike foliage. The autumn colour is not significant. In late spring, it produces 6- to 10-centimetre-wide hemispherical heads of tiny white or pale pink flowers. The plain green-leaved form is not often grown in gardens, as the coloured forms are preferred. Among the oldest is 'Aurea', with yellow foliage. An improvement is 'Dart's Gold' and 'Nugget', both of which have yellow foliage and a more compact habit, 1.8 metres tall. The most dwarf of all is Lemon Candy™, only 70 centimetres tall. 'Diablo', one of the older dark purple selections, has light pink flowers. Summer Wine® is more compact, 1.8 metres tall, with arching stems and nearly black foliage. Fireside® has leaves that are red when they emerge but later turn purple. Little Devil™ has dark purple foliage but its leaves are quite small and the plant only reaches 1.2 metres tall. Tiny Wine® is quite similar but more floriferous. Little Angel™ has reddish purple new growth that matures to deep purple. It

Physocarpus opulifolius Little Devil™.

Physocarpus opulifolius 'Dart's Gold'.

is only 60 centimetres tall. 'Center Glow' has orange-red new foliage that turns reddish purple. Coppertina® has coppery orange foliage, while Amber Jubilee® is a combination of various orange and yellow tones. These last three reach 2.5 metres. Caramel Candy™ has reddish orange new growth maturing to deep green and reaches only 1 metre tall.

Physocarpus opulifolius Coppertina®.

Ninebark, care-free shrubs able to grow in most soil types, organic to rocky, sandy to clay, acidic to alkaline, require only a well-drained site. It is also drought- and salt-tolerant. Although it flowers and, in the case of coloured-leaf forms, performs best in full sun, it is surprisingly shade-tolerant. Ninebark are commonly grown as specimens or in mixed shrub borders, but the dwarf selections are also useful along foundations and even in patio containers. Their salt tolerance means that they perform well in coastal gardens. Pests and diseases are rare. Propagation is by summer or hardwood cuttings. As ninebark are hardy to zone 3, they may be grown throughout Atlantic Canada.

Potentilla fruticosa
SHRUBBY CINQUEFOIL

Among the 300-plus species of *Potentilla* found worldwide, only three are woody types. Because they are woody in nature, these three species were moved to their own genus, *Dasiphora*; however, in the nursery trade, they are still known by their previous name. Shrubby cinquefoil, *P. fruticosa*, is the only one commonly grown as a garden ornamental in Atlantic Canada. This

Potentilla fruticosa 'Abbotswood'.

Potentilla fruticosa 'Pink Beauty'.

plant is found across the northern hemisphere. It varies from being low and matlike to upright and 150 centimetres tall. The leaves are pinnate with no appreciable fall colour. The bark is shredded. The 2- to 3-centimetre-diameter flowers are produced in small terminal clusters from late spring through to fall. Their long blooming season makes them extremely popular landscape shrubs in borders, foundations, roadside medians, and even large rock gardens.

The wild form has bright yellow buttercup-like flowers but modern cultivars come in white and shades of yellow, orange, pink, and red. Over 130 named cultivars are on the market, far too many to describe here. Among the white 1-metre-tall cultivars, 'Abbotswood', 'Mount Everest', and 'White Lady' are the most popular. 'Snowbird' is a double-flowered white cultivar. The shortest are Frosty® and Happy Face® White, at only 60 centimetres. Yellow selections include 'Coronation Triumph', one of the oldest, with bright yellow flowers on 100-centimetre-tall plants. Other bright yellow cultivars which reach similar heights include 'Elizabeth', 'Goldfinger', and Dakota Goldrush®. 'Gold Star', 'Yellow Gem', and Happy Face® Yellow are the shortest yellow cultivars, at 30 to 60 centimetres. 'Yellow Bird' and Citrus Tart® have double yellow flowers on 90-centimetre-tall plants. Cultivars with pale creamy yellow flowers include 'Primrose Beauty', 'Katherine Dyke', and 'Summer Dawn'. Lemon Meringue™ has double, soft yellow flowers with a darker yellow centre. These all reach about 100 centimetres in height, with 'Primrose Beauty' having the bonus of charming silvery foliage. With orange flowers are 'Tangerine', Mango Tango®, and 'Orange Whisper'. 'Setting Sun' is peachy pink with a darker pink eye. Among the pure pink are 'Pink Beauty', 'Pink Whisper', 'Pink Princess', Happy Face® Pink, and Happy Face® Hearts. 'Red Ace' and Marion Red Robin™ are both brick red with orange tones; 'Red Lady' is one of the best truly red cultivars. The orange, pink, and red cultivars are generally 30 to 60 centimetres tall.

Shrubby cinquefoil are adaptable plants. They perform best with full sun and evenly moist soil, but once established, they tolerate drought. They are also well adapted to wind and salt, making them indispensable for coastal gardens. Propagation is by summer cuttings. Hardy to zone 3, they may be grown throughout Atlantic Canada.

Potentilla fruticosa 'Primrose Beauty'.

Prunus X *cistena*.

Prunus
Flowering almond, Nanking cherry

Most species of *Prunus*, more commonly known as cherries, are trees, but a few are small enough to be included among the shrubs. Nanking cherry, *P. tomentosa*, a large shrub, reaching 3 metres in height, is native to northern China, Tibet, and neighbouring Himalayas. Its leaves are elliptical, dark green, with serrated margins, and turn yellow in autumn. In May, just before the leaves unfurl, the stems are smothered in nearly stemless white or pale pink blossoms. These later develop into edible red cherries. Similar in size is double-flowering almond, *P. triloba* 'Multiplex', another Chinese native. Its leaves are elliptical and coarsely toothed but often have two side lobes. Their fall colour is also yellow. Just after the leaves have unfurled in May, they produce fully double pink flowers. This selection is sterile; it does not produce fruit. For smaller gardens, try dwarf flowering almond, *P. glandulosa* 'Sinensis'. It reaches only 1.7 metres, has glossy leaves, and, in May, produces double pink flowers. Unfortunately, this species has no appreciable fall colour. None of the above offer much in summer interest but are valued for their spring blossoms. As all can sucker, use them in the back of a landscape, naturalized or mixed with summer-flowering shrubs. Another noteworthy *Prunus* is purple-leaved sandcherry, *Prunus* X *cistena*. While this shrub has pale pink flowers in May or June, it is mostly grown for its dark purple foliage. Although potentially reaching 3 metres, it is usually pruned to less than 2 metres.

These *Prunus* species require full sun and well-drained, organic-rich soil. They tolerate some drought but not wetness. Related to apples, pears, and plums, they are also prone to fireblight, leaf spot, and powdery mildew. Several moth larvae attack them, as well as borers, aphids, leafhop-

Prunus triloba 'Multiplex'.

pers, and Japanese beetles. Larger browsers can cause damage in winter. Propagation is by summer or hardwood cuttings, or sucker removal. As Nanking cherry and purple-leaved sandcherry are hardy to zone 2 and double-flowering almond to zone 3, both may be grown throughout the region. Dwarf flowering almond is tenderer, rated for zone 4.

Pyracantha coccinea
FIRETHORN

Most *Pyracantha* are native to China but the one species occasionally grown in the mildest areas of Atlantic Canada is firethorn, *P. coccinea*, a native of southern Europe. This very thorny shrub can reach 6 metres in height but in Atlantic Canada it is often less than 3 metres. Normally a broad-leaved evergreen, in Atlantic Canada it is often only semi-evergreen due to its being burnt by winter winds. The narrow, spoon-shaped leaves are glossy green. In June it produces umbels of white flowers which develop into yellow, orange, or red fruit, which remain on the shrub all winter. As firethorn is borderline hardy, it is often grown as an espalier on the south or east side of a building, where it is sheltered from the cold west and northwest winds. In southernmost

Pyracantha coccinea.

Pyracantha coccinea.

Nova Scotia, it may be grown as a living screen or impenetrable informal hedge. Numerous cultivars are available, but the most common are 'Orange Glow' and 'Chadwickii'.

Firethorn prefer full sun, shelter, and fertile but well-drained soil. It is drought-tolerant. Diseases include fireblight and scab; common pests are pear slugs, caterpillars, and aphids. Propagation is by summer or fall cuttings. It is hardy to zone 6.

Pyracantha coccinea.

Rhus
Sumac

About 35 species of sumac are scattered across the northern hemisphere, but only two are regularly grown as a garden ornamental in North America. The largest is *Rhus typhina* or the staghorn sumac, a large shrub or small tree reaching 8 metres in height, native throughout the Maritimes. The wild form, with large compound leaves, fuzzy stems, decorative rusty seed heads (on female plants), and scarlet fall colour can be used in a naturalized setting, but, with its suckering habit, it is a little coarse for most gardens. More decorative is the selection 'Dissecta', also known as 'Laciniata', whose leaflets are further divided into more leaflets, resulting in lacy foli-

Rhus typhina Tiger Eyes®.

Rhus typhina Tiger Eyes®.

Ribes sanguineum 'King Edward VII'.

age. It is generally less than 5 metres tall but it can still sucker. The most striking is 'Bailtiger', more commonly known as Tiger Eyes®, a yellow-foliaged sport of 'Laciniata' that matures at 2 metres tall and is far less aggressive. Fragrant sumac, *R. aromatica*, a suckering shrub reaching 1.2 to 2 metres, has trifoliate leaves; the leaves and stems are fragrant when bruised. 'Gro-low', a dwarf, wide-spreading selection, reaches 60 centimetres tall but up to 2 metres wide. It is perhaps best used as a ground cover on embankments. Both sumacs have exceptional fall colour in shades of yellow, orange, and red.

To obtain the best fall colour, grow sumac in full sun; however, they do tolerate part shade. The soil should be well drained; they do not tolerate soggy soil. Sumac are adaptable to variable soil pH. Once established, both species are drought-tolerant. Sumac is ideal for naturalized landscapes or as a backdrop in shrub borders. Tiger Eyes® is a wonderful shrub to grow as a specimen. *Rhus* are generally not bothered by insects, browsers, or disease, although leaf spot and mildew may occur when plants are grown in sheltered locations. Propagation is by sucker removal or by root cuttings. As both species are rated hardy to zone 3, they can be grown throughout Atlantic Canada.

Ribes
FLOWERING CURRANT

The genus *Ribes* includes currants and gooseberries, but two species are grown primarily for their ornamental value. Golden or buffalo currant, *R. aureum*, is native to the western half of North America. It forms a loose shrub, 1.5 to 2 metres tall. Its thornless stems have glossy three-lobed leaves that turn reddish purple in autumn. The trumpet-shaped, yellow, clove-scented flowers are produced in drooping clusters in May-June. It produces edible, amber-coloured berries. From the Pacific Northwest is red-flowering currant, *R. sanguineum*. Thornless, it too can reach 2.5 to 3 metres tall, with three- to five-lobed dull green leaves but no appreciable fall colour. It has drooping clusters of reddish pink flowers, up to 8 centimetres in length, in May or June. 'King Edward VII' has reddish pink flowers on a more compact plant usually less than 2 metres. 'Pulborough Scarlet' has two-tone red and white flowers; 'White Icicle' is white. They produce

Ribes sanguineum 'King Edward VII'.

blue edible but insipid fruit. These flowering currants are useful along foundations, naturalized settings, and wildflower gardens or mixed with other shrubs. They attract hummingbirds, bees, and butterflies.

Alpine currant, *R. alpinum*, from northern Eurasia, is grown primarily as a hedge plant. Its flowers are insignificant, but the three- to five-lobed leaves are small and glossy. It may be used as a 1- to 2-metre-high hedge and is perhaps the best hedging material for shady or cold locations.

Both flowering currants bloom best with full sun but tolerate part shade. Red-flowering currant prefers evenly moist soil that is reasonably fertile; golden currant tolerates dry, poor rocky soil. Golden currant prefers alkaline soil. Alpine currant tolerates full sun to full shade and has some drought tolerance. Pests are mostly sawfly larvae or aphids. Diseases include leaf spot, rust, and powdery mildew. Propagation is by summer or hardwood cuttings. Alpine currant is hardy to zone 2, golden currant to zone 4, and red-flowering currant to zone 6, and only suitable in milder parts of Atlantic Canada.

Rosa
ROSES

Entire books have been devoted to growing roses so, for simplicity, only the hardiest shrub roses will be described here. By far the easiest to grow in Atlantic Canada is rugose rose, *Rosa rugosa*. This rose is native to coastal regions of northern Japan, adjacent northern China, and eastern Russia. We have grown this species of rose in Atlantic Canada for over 100 years, and it is now naturalized in many parts of the region. While it is a little coarse for a refined rose garden, it is perhaps the hardiest rose. Rugose rose is a suckering, thorny shrub that can reach 2 metres in height. The leaves are glossy and heavily veined. In autumn, they turn brilliant yellow and may be orange-red on some plants. The highly fragrant flowers, up to 10 centimetres wide, are rose pink on the wild species; modern selections are available in shades of pink, pur-

RIGHT: *Rosa* 'Albertine' and 'Champlain'.
BELOW: *Rosa* 'Evelyn'.

ple, or white, often with semi-double or double flowers. Blooming starts in early summer but can continue sporadically into late summer. In fall, attractive orange-red hips are produced, which often remain on the plant all winter. Suggested cultivars include 'Hansa' (double reddish pink), 'Blanc Double de Coubert' (double white), 'Frau Dagmar Hastrup' (single pink), 'Therese Bugnet' (double light pink), 'Grootendorst Pink' (clusters of small double pink carnation-like flowers), and 'F. J. Grootendorst' (like previous but reddish pink flowers).

Highly recommended for Atlantic Canada are the Canadian-bred Explorer roses. Originally bred by Agriculture Canada in Ottawa, then L'Assumption, Quebec, this group of hardy shrub roses were bred for resistance to many common rose diseases. Not surprisingly, *Rosa rugosa* features as a parent in many hybrids. Pop-

Rosa rugosa 'Blanc Double de Coubert'.

ular cultivars include 'Martin Frobisher' (light pink), 'William Baffin' (cherry red), 'Henry Hudson' (white), 'David Thompson' (deep pink), 'Champlain' (red), 'Henry Kelsey' (climber, deep pink), 'John Cabot' (climber, cherry red), and 'John Davis' (climber, pink). This rose-breeding program continues to be carried out by the Vineland Research Station in Guelph, under the Canadian Artist series. 'Campfire' is perhaps the most popular, with flowers a blend of yellow and pink. Other shrub roses that are doing well in Atlantic Canada are the Parkland and David Austin roses.

Rugose rose prefer acidic soil but tolerate adverse soil conditions such as clay soil, sandy soil, and drought. Full sun is best, but it tolerates part shade. However, it does not tolerate wet soil. It has excellent salt tolerance, which makes it indispensable for planting in coastal gardens. Propagation is by summer cuttings, hardwood cuttings, or sucker divisions. Explorer roses are tough but not as sensitive to soil pH variation. Both groups are relatively disease-free, although powdery mildew can be a problem if plants are grown in a too sheltered site. They may be attacked by aphids, pear slugs, leafrollers, or Japanese beetles. Rugose rose is super hardy to zone 2, while most Explorer roses are hardy to zones 3 or 4.

Rosa 'Leander'.

Rubus
Flowering raspberry, thimbleberry

We often think of raspberry as spiny-stemmed plants with delicious red berries. But three raspberry are grown solely for their ornamental flowers. Naturalized in the Maritimes is *R. odoratus*, the purple-flowered raspberry. It is a suckering shrub 1 to 2 metres tall with relatively large maplelike leaves that turn yellow in autumn. In June and July, plants produce clusters of 3- to 5-centimetre-wide purple-pink flowers that turn into flattened, mealy, red raspberry-like fruit. From western North America are two ornamental species. *Rubus spectabilis* resembles *R. odoratus* but has smaller flowers. The cultivar 'Olympic Rose' has fully double flowers. Thimbleberry, *R. parviflorus*, another look-alike, has single white flowers. Difficult to find in Atlantic Canada is *Rubus* 'Benenden', a popular European ornamental that can reach 2 to 3 metres tall. In June it produces 8-centimetre-diameter white flowers. From a distance, it looks like a rose shrub.

The above *Rubus* grow in sun to shade in any reasonably moist, acidic, fertile soil. Pests and diseases are rare, although powdery mildew may occur occasionally. Propagation is by seed or suckers. As both sucker prolifically, they are best used in naturalized settings such as embankments or under taller trees. They are good bee plants. As *Rubus odoratus* and *R. parviflora* are hardy to zone 2, they may be grown throughout Atlantic Canada; *Rubus spectabilis* is tender, hardy to zone 4, and R. 'Benenden' to zone 5.

Rubus spectabilis 'Olympic Rose'.

Rubus odoratus.

Rubus 'Benenden'.

TODD BOLAND

Salix
WILLOW

Willows are one of the largest plant genera. Many are tall trees but quite a few are ornamental shrubs grown for their foliage, bark, or catkins. Perhaps the most decorative for foliage is *Salix integra* 'Hakuro Nishiki' or 'Flamingo'. Both have thin stems and narrow leaves irregularly blotched with white and pink. New growth is particularly bright pink. It can reach 175 centimetres tall and is usually grown as a lawn specimen. *Salix cinerea* 'Variegata', similar but with stiffer branches, can reach 3 to 6 metres in height. Grown for its bright yellow foliage is *S. sachalinensis* 'Golden Sunshine', a fast-growing large shrub which can reach 5 metres. Arctic willow, *S. purpurea* 'Gracilis' has blue-tinted foliage and a dense 125-centimetre-tall habit, making it ideal for hedging purposes.

With elegant silver-white leaves are *S. repens*

Salix candida Iceberg Alley™.

'Argentea', *S. helvatica*, and *S. candida* Iceberg Alley™. The former has prostrate stems, 60 centimetres high but spreading over 2 metres wide,

Salix integra 'Hakuro-nishiki'.

making it suitable as a ground cover. *Salix helvatica* is a small rounded shrub up to 60 centimetres tall. Iceberg Alley™, an introduction from the Memorial University of Newfoundland Botanical Garden in St. John's, is an upright shrub up to 120 centimetres tall with magnificent silvery white leaves.

Grown for their winter stems are *S. alba* 'Britzensis' and 'Flame'. The former has red stems, the latter orange-yellow. Both reach 150 centimetres tall. Grown for their decorative silvery spring catkins are *S. discolor*, a native 5-metre-tall shrub, or *S. caprea* 'Pendula', a top-grafted weeping form of French pussywillow. For something different, *S. gracilistyla* 'Melanostachys' has unique black catkins and reaches 2 metres.

Several willows are ideal as ground covers on embankments or cascading over retaining walls. One of the best is *Salix lindleyana*, which has tiny, shiny leaves and small pink catkins. Similar and equally desirable is *S. myrtilloides* 'Pink Tassels'.

Salix gracilistyla 'Melanostachys'.

With a creeping habit is also *S. nakamurana* var. *yezo-alpina*, which has relatively large, round leaves and large silvery catkins.

Willows are lovers of moisture and fertile soil. They do not tolerate drought or roadside or coastal salt spray. Willows are regularly attacked by wood borers, moth larvae, and aphids; they are also plagued by blights, leaf spot, cankers, and powdery mildew. They are commonly browsed by herbivores. As a consolation, they grow rapidly and can sometimes rebound from these pests and diseases. Propagation is by summer or hardwood cuttings. *Salix discolor*, *S. candida*, and *S. repens* are hardy to zone 2; *S. alba*, zone 3; and the remainder, zone 4.

Sambucus
ELDERBERRY

There are about 25 species of *Sambucus*, with worldwide distribution. As a group, they are large multi-stemmed shrubs with large pinnate leaves and clusters of white flowers that develop into small berries commonly consumed by birds. Several species, along with numerous cultivars, are commonly grown as ornamentals in temperate gardens. Native to Europe is the black elderberry, *S. nigra*. In eastern North America is the similar American black elderberry, *S. canadensis*, referred to as *S. nigra* ssp. *canadensis* by some taxonomists. Both reach 3 to 4 metres tall and have flat-topped clusters of scented flowers in June or July, followed by edible black berries. Several cultivars are grown primarily for fruit production: 'York', 'Adams 1', 'Adams 2', 'Kent', 'Nova', 'Scotia' and 'Victoria'. As obvious by the cultivar names, several of these were developed in Nova Scotia. These edible types have plain green foliage. From an ornamental point of view, the most popular is 'Aurea', which has golden yellow foliage. 'Aureovariegata', 'Madonna', and

Sambucus nigra 'Madonna'.
PREVIOUS SPREAD: *Sambucus nigra* 'Black Lace'.

Instant Karma® have white to yellow-edged leaves, while 'Pulverulenta' has white mottled leaves. Quite striking is 'Guincho Purple' which has purple foliage and pale pink flowers; Black Beauty®, which has darker purple foliage; and Black Lace®, which has deeply cut lacy purple foliage. For restricted spaces, try Black Tower®, a fastigiated form (narrow, upright growth habit) of Black Beauty®. From western North America is *S. caerulea*, sometimes referred to as *S. nigra* ssp. *caerulea*. While this plant has green leaves, the berries are an attractive powder blue.

Native across the northern hemisphere, including Atlantic Canada, is red elderberry, *S. racemosa* (includes *S. pubens*). This 3- to 4-metre-tall shrub produces conical clusters of creamy white flowers in May, followed by bright red berries in July and August. Unlike the previous species, the red elderberry does not have edible berries. 'Plumosa Aurea' has deeply cut bright yellow foliage. 'Sutherland Gold' has even more lacy foliage. Lemony Lace™ is a dwarf 1.6-metre-tall cultivar with lacy-cut leaves. 'Golden Glow', also 1.6 metres tall, has red-tinted spring leaves that later turn yellow. 'Goldenlocks' has yellow leaves with lacy-cut but very narrow leaflets.

Elderberries prefer organic-rich, evenly moist, well-drained soil. It is adaptable to variations in soil pH. They do tolerate wet soil. Full sun develops the best foliar colour on the yellow- and purple-leaved cultivars, but part shade is tolerated. For the cultivars with decorative leaves, hard-pruning is recommended every few years. This keeps the plants compact and less woody. Their fragile branches can be damaged by heavy snow load. Use elderberries as specimens or living screens or at the back of a shrub border. They are also useful for naturalized settings or damp depressions. The main disease is powdery mildew, if its location is too sheltered; cankers and leaf spot also occur. While few insects bother them, elder borer beetle can be particularly devastating. Propagation is by summer and hardwood cuttings. Red elderberry is hardy to zone 3; black elderberry, to zone 4.

Skimmia japonica
JAPANESE SKIMMIA

The four species of *Skimmia* are all native to East Asia, where they grow as understory shrubs. *S. japonica* is rarely seen in Atlantic Canada but is hardy enough for the milder areas of the region. It forms a rounded mound up to 1.2 metres tall, with lance-shaped, deep green evergreen leaves that are slightly aromatic when bruised. Plants are dioecious; both sexes produce rounded terminal clusters of fragrant white flowers in May or June. Female plants will develop clusters of red berries that often stay on the plant through much of the winter. 'Rubella', a compact male clone that reaches 75 centimetres tall, has red buds that form in the fall and look attractive all

Skimmia japonica.

winter. Attractive introductions from Holland include Red Dwarf®, Pink Dwarf®, and White Dwarf® male clones, which have red, pink, or creamy yellow winter buds on compact rounded plants. These are ideal as pot plants for patios. Among the female clones are 'Nymans', which forms a larger plant; 'Chameleon', whose berries change from green to white to red; and 'Pabella', which is compact with abundant fruit production. 'Reevesiana', a hermaphroditic form which has both male and female flowers, produce fruit even as a stand-alone plant. However, fruit production is better if a male plant is nearby. 'Temptation' is a more compact hermaphroditic form. For decorative foliage try Magic Marlot® or Mystic Marlot®, both of which have grey-green leaves with a white margin, both compact male plants with red overwintering buds.

Skimmia prefer well-drained, humus-rich, acidic soil in part to full shade; in fact, it is one of the most shade-tolerant shrubs. Too much sun results in scorched leaves. It is surprisingly drought-tolerant. It is a lovely subject for shrub borders, foundation plantings, and woodland settings. It is not bothered by pests or diseases. Propagation is by summer cuttings. As it is rated hardy to zone 6, it can only be grown in the milder areas of Atlantic Canada, particularly southern Nova Scotia and southern Newfoundland.

Sorbaria sorbifolia
Ural false spirea

Sorbaria sorbifolia, or Ural false spirea, has been grown in Atlantic Canada for so long it is considered a heritage or heirloom plant. It can reach 3 metres but is more commonly 2 metres in height. The foliage is compound with serrated leaflets, similar to those of mountain-ash, *Sorbus*. The fall foliage turns yellow. In July, false spirea produces dense, arching, pyramidal clusters of small white flowers, up to 25 centimetres long. This shrub suckers with abandon: use it with caution. However, for naturalized settings, roadsides, or embankments, it is an easy, rapidly spreading shrub. The cultivar 'Sem' has notable pink- to purple-tinted spring foliage.

False spirea grow in sun or part shade and any reasonably moist, fertile soil. It has few pests or diseases. Propagation is by sucker removal. Hardy to zone 2, it can be grown almost anywhere in Atlantic Canada.

Sorbaria sorbifolia.

Sorbus cashmiriana.

Sorbus frutescens.

Sorbus
MOUNTAIN-ASH

Most gardeners are familiar with mountain-ash. This medium-height tree is both native to Atlantic Canada and popular as a garden ornamental, valued mostly for its large clusters of orange-red fruit. However, this genus of over 60 species has several dwarf shrubby species that are welcome additions to Atlantic Canadians gardens, if you can track them down. The most likely species to be found is *Sorbus reducta*. A miniature mountain-ash, it reaches only 1 metre tall. Small pinnate leaves turn chocolate-purple in autumn. Clusters of white flowers develop into crimson fruit that later turn white, often with pink flecks. Occasionally seen is *S. frutescens*, erroneously labelled *S. koehneana* in some books. This upright shrub can reach 2 metres in height. Its foliage is like that of a miniature mountain-ash, with fall colour an admirable mix of yellow, orange, red, and purple. Its white flowers develop into snow-white fruit that often remain well into winter.

Other dwarf mountain-ash less than 3 metres tall include *S. cashmiriana*, *S. filipes*, *S. gonggashanica*, *S. bissetii*, and the hybrid 'Molly Sanderson'. All have excellent fall foliage and white fruit that remain on the plant through much of the winter.

Dwarf mountain-ash prefer full sun and organic-rich, fertile soil that is well drained. The above prefer slightly acidic soil. Pests and diseases are not common, but they are susceptible to fireblight and may be attacked by leafrollers. As young plants may be browsed by hares, they require protection in rural settings. Propagation is by seed. The above are all hardy to zone 5.

Spiraea
SPIREA

The nearly 100 species of *Spiraea* are all native to the northern hemisphere, with the majority in Asia. They are extremely popular as garden ornamentals. It is the rare garden that does not have at least one. Those we grow in Atlantic Canada fall into two main groups—the lower-growing pink-flowered *S. japonica* hybrids and the upright, white-flowered types. The Japanese spirea, *S. japonica*, is often sold as *S.* X *bumalda*. It is a dense, mounding shrub with small oval toothed leaves and flat-topped clusters of tiny pink flowers from late June through July and scattered through to autumn. Popular cultivars include 'Froebelii' (red-tinted spring leaves, deep pink flowers, wine red fall colour, 120 centimetres), 'Anthony Waterer' (as 'Froebelii' but carmine red flowers, 90 centimetres), 'Dart's Red' (as 'Anthony Waterer' but even darker red), 'Goldflame' (orange spring foliage turns yellow, pink flowers, 120 centimetres), 'Shirobana' (unique blend of white, pink, and carmine flowers, 90 centimetres), 'Neon Flash' (bright cherry red, 90 centimetres), 'Goldmound' (as 'Goldflame', but 75 centimetres), 'Flaming Mound' (as 'Goldmound', but bright orange new growth), and 'Little Princess' (pink, 75 centimetres). All are popular as foundation plants, informal hedges, or mixed in a shrub border. For smaller gardens, try the 60-centimetre-tall Double Play® series or the 30-centimetre-tall Carpet® series; these are small enough to use in rock-garden settings. One last noteworthy cultivar is Double Play® Painted Lady®. This 60-centimetre-tall cultivar's pink flowers contrast with leaves irregularly streaked and striped with yellow.

Many white-flowered spirea are available. The earliest to bloom is baby's-breath spirea, *S. thunbergii*, which blooms May-June on 1.7-metre-tall shrubs. The flowers are produced on arching branches. 'Ogon' is a selection with bright yellow foliage. Very similar to baby's-breath spirea

Spirea X *bumalda* 'Goldmound'.

Spiraea X *vanhouttei* 'Renaissance'.

Spiraea betulifolia 'Tor'.

is garland spirea, *S.* X *arguta*, which can reach 2.5 metres. The selection 'Compacta' will be half the height. The Vanhoutte or bridalwreath spirea, *S.* X *vanhouttei* 'Renaissance', blooms a couple of weeks later and has white rounded clusters of flowers on 2.5-metre-tall shrubs. Similar but smaller, with trilobed leaves, is *S. trilobata*, which reaches 1.2 metres. Next to bloom is the snowmound spirea, *S. nipponicum* 'Snowmound', which also has white rounded clusters of flowers on 1.2-metre-tall plants. 'Halward's Silver' is smaller at 100 centimetres in height. The last of the white-flowered spirea to bloom, in late June into July, is the birch-leaved spirea, *S. betulifolia*. 'Tor' is the most popular cultivar, a dense mound reaching 120 centimetres tall and even wider with time. Of the above white-flowered types, it is the only one with attractive fall colour, in this case orange-yellow. Glow Girl® has golden yellow summer foliage; Pink Sparkles™ has pink flowers.

Spirea prefer full sun and fertile but well-drained soil that is slightly acidic. Alkaline soil can lead to chlorosis. Part shade is tolerated, but flowering will be compromised. Spirea are not particularly drought- or salt-tolerant. All spirea are excellent bee and butterfly plants. The most serious disease is powdery mildew; aphids and leafrollers are the most common insect pests.

Propagation is by summer or hardwood cuttings. Japanese spirea are hardy to zone 3; the white-flowered types are best in zone 4 or milder.

Stephanandra incisa
LACE SHRUB

Only one species of *Stephanandra* is grown in Atlantic Canada, *Stephanandra incisa*, a native of Japan and Korea. It forms a low but spreading shrub, 60 centimetres tall but 2 metres wide. The arching stems have small maplelike leaves that are bright green in summer and turn a superb orange-yellow in autumn. These stems often root where they touch the ground, resulting in a ground-cover effect. It is suitable for a mixed

Stephanandra incisa 'Crispa'.

Stephanandra incisa 'Crispa'.

shrub border but also useful for cascading over retaining walls or as a ground cover on embankments. Throughout the summer, plants produce small rounded clusters of white starlike flowers. 'Crispa', the standard cultivar grown, is noted for its deep-cut leaves.

Stephanandra prefer acidic, humus-rich soil that stays reasonably moist. Full sun produces the most flowers and best fall colour, but part shade is tolerated. Plants respond well to shearing. Propagation is by summer cuttings. It is not bothered by any serious pests or diseases. It is hardy to zone 5.

Symphoricarpos
SNOWBERRY, CORALBERRY

Fifteen species fall within the genus *Symphoricarpos*; all are from North America, except one species from western China. The genus name comes from the Greek *symphorein*, together, and *karpos*, fruit, in reference to the berries appearing in clusters. While still widely grown, *S. albus*, the common snowberry or waxberry, is rarely offered in local nurseries. However, many gardens throughout Atlantic Canada still grow this suckering shrub, most often as a hedge or screen. It is now naturalized across Atlantic Canada. If untrimmed, it can reach 2 metres in height, with quickly spreading suckers. The rounded, paired leaves are often tinted blue or grey; they have no appreciable fall colour. The small, pink, bell-shaped flowers are produced in terminal clusters in July, followed by white berries in autumn. The berries often remain well into the winter months.

More attractive are the coralberries. They are similar to snowberry but produce pink to purplish berries. They generally reach 1.2 to 1.5 metres tall. Amethyst™ (hot pink), 'Scarlet Pearl' (purple-pink), 'Magic Berry' (lilac-pink), Charming Fantasy™ (blush pink), and *S. orbicu-*

Symphoricarpos albus.

Symphoricarpos orbiculatus.

latus (purple-red) are suggested cultivars and species. Reaching only 50 centimetres in height is *S.* X *chenaultii* 'Hancock', with dark pink berries.

Snowberry and coralberry prefer full sun and well-drained soil. They tolerate poor soil, some drought, and even shade, but fruit production will be reduced. As they are related to honeysuckle, *Lonicera*, they are prone to many of the same infestations, mainly by moth caterpillars. Powdery mildew and leaf spot are also possible. Propagation is by sucker removal or summer or hardwood cuttings. Snowberry and coralberry are hardy to zone 3.

Syringa
LILAC

All lilacs are native to Eurasia. In theory, all the species can be grown in Atlantic Canada, but not all are available in local nurseries. By far the most popular is the common lilac, *Syringa vulgaris*, a European native. As it has been grown for over 100 years in Atlantic Canada, it qualifies as a heirloom or heritage plant. Common lilac can reach 5 metres tall and typically has highly fragrant, 15- to 20-centimetre-long pyramidal clusters of lilac purple, four-petalled flowers from late May through June. 'Alba' is the white-flowered form. More popular cultivars include 'Charles Joly' (lilac-pink), 'Sensation' (two-tone reddish purple and white), 'President Lincoln' (porcelain blue), 'Sarah Sands' (reddish purple), 'Ludwig Spaeth' (reddish purple), 'Primrose' (pale yellow), 'President Grevy' (double-flowered lilac-blue), 'Beauty of Moscow' (double-flowered pale pink), and 'Madame Lemoine' (double-flowered white). 'Aucubaefolia' has attractive yellow-mottled foliage and lilac-blue flowers. For limited space, try 'Wonderblue', a lavender-blue selection that is less than 2 metres tall.

For large gardens try Hungarian lilac, *S. josikaea*; nodding lilac, *S. komorowii* ssp. *reflexa*; and their hybrid, *S.* X *josiflexa*. All reach 5 to 6 metres tall and up to 10 metres wide. They flower a couple of weeks later than the common lilac and have nodding panicles of reddish purple to lilac purple flowers that fade to pale shades as they age.

Syringa komorowii ssp. *reflexa*.
RIGHT: *Syringa vulgaris*.

Similar in size to common lilac are the Preston lilacs, *S.* X *prestoniae* (*komorovii* X *villosa*) and early-flowering lilac, *S.* X *hyacinthiflora* (*oblata* X *vulgaris*). Preston lilacs bloom just after common lilac. Popular cultivars include 'Donald Wyman' (lilac purple), 'Minuet' (light purple), 'Miss Canada' (rosy pink), 'Isabella' (lavender-pink), 'James Macfarlane' (pink), and 'Red Wine' (reddish purple). Early flowering lilac blooms just before the common lilac. The most popular cultivars are 'Pocahontas' (reddish purple), 'Sweetheart' (double-flowered lavender-pink), 'Mount Baker' (white), 'Anabel' (double-flowered pink), 'Dark Knight' (purple), and 'Maiden's Blush' (pale pink). All are grown as specimen plants or living screens.

The remaining lilac are smaller statured, generally about 2 metres tall, with smaller foliage and flowers. These are popular as foundation plants or for use in smaller gardens. Popular among these are Korean lilac, *S. pubescens* ssp. *patula* 'Miss Kim' (2 metres, lavender purple); dwarf Korean lilac, *S. meyeri* 'Palibin' (1.7 metres, lavender purple); *S. meyeri* Tinkerbelle® (1.7 metres, pink); and the Bloomerang® series (1.7 metres, pink to deep purple), the last notable for repeat blooms later in the season. Josee™, 'Colby's Wishing Star', 'Red Pixie', and Scent and Sensibility™ are similar dwarf repeat-blooming hybrids. For something different, try the pinnate-leaved lilac, *S. pinnatifolia*. Its foliage is like that of a small-leaved ash—unlike a typical lilac, which has elliptical to heart-shaped leaves. The flowers are produced in small, pale lavender trusses on a plant reaching 2.5 metres in height.

All lilac prefer full sun and alkaline, well-

Syringa X *prestoniae* 'Donald Wyman'.

Syringa vulgaris 'Sarah Sands'.

Tamarix ramosissima.

drained reasonably fertile soil. For those gardening with acidic soil, a yearly dusting of lime is beneficial. Butterflies and hummingbirds readily nectar from the blossoms. The main pest is leaf miner, which can cause considerable cosmetic damage. Blights and powdery mildew are the main diseases. Propagation is by summer cuttings. All the above are hardy to zone 3, so they may be grown throughout Atlantic Canada.

Tamarix
Salt-cedar

The over 50 species of *Tamarix* found worldwide are natives of Eurasia and Africa. Only one is grown in Atlantic Canada, *T. ramosissima*, commonly called salt-cedar. This tall shrub can reach 3 to 5 metres tall. The foliage is scalelike, similar to that of cedar, hence the common name. Tiny pink blossoms clothe the stems in July and August. 'Pink Cascade' is perhaps the most popular cultivar. This shrub responds well to hard-pruning; if it gets too rangy, it may be pruned to within a few feet of the ground and will flush up new growth.

Tamarix, a sun and heat lover, prefer sandy soils. Excellent drought and salt tolerance make it popular for coastal gardens. It is practically pest- and disease-free. Propagation is by seed or summer cuttings. It is rated hardy to zone 3 but, with its love of summer heat, it generally does not perform well in Newfoundland.

Tamarix ramosissima.

Viburnum X bodnantense 'Dawn'.

Viburnum
VIBURNUM

The more than 150 species of *Viburnum* are native across the northern hemisphere. As a group, they have opposite leaves and flat-topped clusters of white to pink flowers followed by small berrylike drupes that attract fruit-eating birds. Those from northern areas are deciduous, often with magnificent fall colour, while those from southern areas are broad-leaved evergreens. Numerous species and cultivars are grown in temperate gardens. The earliest to bloom are *V. grandiflorum*, *V. farreri*, and their hybrid, *V.* X *bodnantense*. These all have elliptical, ribbed foliage and nodding clusters of highly fragrant pink flowers in winter to mid-spring, usually blooming before leaves appear. All reach 3 metres tall, except *V. farreri* 'Nanum', which reaches about 1 metre. Among *V.* X *bodnantense* cultivars are 'Pink Dawn', 'Charles Lamont', and 'Deben', the latter with white rather than pink flowers.

Among eastern North American wild viburnums are witherod, *V. nudum* and *V. cassinoides*. Both reach 4 metres in height and have glossy elliptical to lance-shaped leaves, flat-topped clusters of creamy white flowers in early summer followed by fruit that change from green to pink then blue-black. Fall colour is a mix of yellow and wine red. Brandywine™, 'Pink Beauty', and 'Winterthur' are the most popular cultivars. Similar but larger is nannyberry, *V. lentago*, which reaches 5 metres; rusty nannyberry, *V. rufidulum*, 6 metres; and blackhaw viburnum, *V. prunifolium*, 6 metres. Also native to eastern North America is arrowwood, *V. dentatum*. This shrub reaches 3 metres and has ovate leaves that are ribbed with serrated margins. Clusters of white flowers produced in late spring become blue-black fruit in

Viburnum lantana.

autumn. Fall colour is a mix of yellow, orange, and red. Blue Muffin® was selected for its appealing powder blue fruit on a compact 1.6-metre plant. Chicago Lustre ® and All that Glitters® have superb glossy foliage, while Autumn Jazz® was selected for its outstanding fall foliage. Bracted viburnum, *V. bracteatum* All that Glows®, reaches 2 metres and has blue-black fruit and glossy ovate leaves. Hobblebush, *V. lantanoides*, is yet another eastern North American native. This 4-metre shrub has heart-shaped ribbed foliage and clusters of white flowers in late spring, followed by red fruit in fall. The European wayfaring tree, *V. lantana*, can grow 5 metres tall and has oval to elliptical foliage that is densely hairy on the undersides. Hemispherical clusters of all fertile creamy white flowers develop into red fruit. 'Mohican', a compact cultivar, reaches 2.5 metres.

European highbush cranberry, *V. opulus*, and American highbush cranberry, *V. trilobum* (now known as *V. opulus* var. *trilobum*), both reach 4 metres and are grown for their white flowers, attractive red fruit (edible on *V. trilobumetres*), and splendid red fall colour. These viburnums have a combination of smaller fertile flowers surrounded by larger sterile ones. Snowball bush, *Viburnum opulus* 'Roseum' (aka 'Sterile'), has all sterile flowers held in a globular cluster, but it does not produce fruit.

A number of garden-worthy viburnums hail from Asia. Leatherleaf viburnum, *V. rhytidophyllum*, can reach 3 metres tall and has elliptical to lance-shaped, wrinkled, leathery leaves that are semi-evergreen. White flowers produce red fruit that eventually turn black. 'Cree' is a popular, slightly hardier cultivar. The hybrid between leatherleaf viburnum and wayfaring tree, *V.* X *rhytidophylloides*, is similar to leatherleaf viburnum but more deciduous. 'Alleghany' and 'Willowwood' are popular cultivars. The newer Red Balloon® was selected for its better fruit set. Linden viburnum, *V. dilatatum*, reaches 3 metres and has rounded foliage, white flowers, and red

Viburnum X carlecephalum.

Viburnum plicatum 'Mariesii'.

fruit. It has admirable fall colour in a blend of red, bronze, and burgundy. 'Erie', 'Catskill', and 'Asian Beauty' are popular cultivars, while Cardinal Candy® is a dwarf, free-fruiting selection reaching 1.6 metres. *V. dilatatum* hybrids include 'Emerald Triumph', 'Oneida', and 'Fugitive'. Siebold's viburnum, *V. sieboldii*, reaches 6 metres and has white flowers and fruit that changes from red to black. Doublefile viburnum, *V. plicatum*, has ovate leaves with sharply toothed margins. Like highbush cranberry, its flowers are also composed of small fertile inner flowers that are surrounded by larger sterile flowers. Its fruit is red. Reaching 4 metres tall and often even wider, this species has distinct layered branches that add architectural elements to the landscape. 'Mariesii' is the most popular cultivar; 'Shasta' is more dwarf, at 2.5 metres; 'Watanabei' is even smaller, at 2 metres. 'Summer Snowflake', at 2.5 metres, has its main flower flush in late spring but blooms sporadically all summer. 'Sterile', at 5 metres, and 'Popcorn', at 2.5 metres, have all sterile flowers held in a rounded cluster that looks similar to the common snowball bush. With a combination of sterile and fertile flowers is also the Chinese species *V. sargentii*. 'Onondaga', a popular selection, it reaches 2 metres and has purple-red buds opening to pale pink fertile flowers and white sterile flowers.

Of Asian origin are also the fragrant snowball viburnums. The most important species is Koreanspice viburnum, *V. carlesii*, whose pink buds open to white, highly fragrant snowball-like clusters in late spring. Their leaves are rounded and covered in stiff hairs. Hybrids developed from *V. carlesii* include *V.* X *juddii* (*carlesii* X *bitchiuense*), *V.* X *burkwoodii* (*utile* X *carlesii*), *V.* X *carlecephalum* (*carlesii* X *macrocephalum*), and 'Eskimo'. All

Viburnum opulus 'Compactus'.

are similar, reaching 2 to 3 metres with white, fragrant, round flower clusters. *Viburnum* X *pragense* (*utile* X *rhytidophyllum*) is similar but has semi-evergreen glossy foliage and round but only slightly fragrant flower clusters.

Viburnum prefer evenly moist, highly organic, well-drained soil. They adapt to a variety of soil pH levels. Full sun develops the best flowers, most fruit, and optimal fall colour, but part shade is tolerated. As many are partly self-sterile, better fruit production occurs when two or more plants are grown near each other. Propagation is by summer or hardwood cuttings. The most serious pest is viburnum leaf beetle, which, after several years of attack, completely destroys the plant. Thin-leaved viburnums such as *V. opulus*, *V. plicatum*, and *V. dentatum* are the most susceptible. Powdery mildew can attack all of them if the site is too sheltered. Hardiness is variable among the species and hybrids. *Viburnum opulus* is hardy to zone 2; *V. lentago*, *V. cassinoides*, *V. prunifolium*, and *V. dentatum*, zone 3; *V. lanatana*, *V. lantanoides*, and *V. sieboldii*, zone 4; all the fragrant snowballs, *V.* X *bodnantense*, *V. dilatatum*, *V. nudum*, *V. rufidulum*, *V. plicatum*, and the leatherleaf types, rated for zone 5; and *V. bracteatum*, zone 6.

Weigela
WEIGELA

Weigela are among the most popular flowering shrubs in Atlantic Canada. This genus, native to East Asia, was named for German scientist and botanist Christian Ehrenfried Weigel (1748–1831). The main species grown in Atlantic Canada is *W. florida*. The wild form can reach over 3 metres tall but many modern cultivars are less than 2 metres. Plants have paired elliptical leaves but no appreciable fall colour. The funnel-shaped flowers are rose pink, 4 centimetres long, and produced in clusters in June and July, with scattered flowers throughout the rest of the season. Having been grown for over 100 years, there have been many selections, ranging in colour from shades of pink and red, as well as white. Some of the older cultivars, reaching 1.5 metres or taller, are 'Bristol Ruby' (red), 'Bristol Snowflake' (white), 'Pink Princess', 'Red Prince', and 'Abel Carriere' (white to pink). Bred in Canada are the Dance™ series, compact 6- to 90-centimetre-tall cultivars: 'Minuet' (red), 'Rumba' (reddish pink), 'Polka' (two-tone pink),

Weigela florida 'Bristol Ruby'.

Weigela florida 'Variegata'.
LEFT: *Weigela florida* 'Minuet'.

and 'Tango' (light pink). Ever-blooming weigela include the Sonic Bloom® series, reaching 120 to 150 centimetres; the Czechmark® and Date Night™ series, reaching 100 to 130 centimetres; and the dwarf Snippet® series, reaching just 60 centimetres.

The oldest variegated cultivar is 'Variegata', which reaches 2 metres, with white-edged leaves and pink flowers. French Lace™, also tall, has yellow-edged leaves and red flowers. My Monet® and My Monet® 'Sunset' have white and yellow-edged leaves respectively on plants less than 45 centimetres tall but do not produce many blooms. With pure yellow leaves is 'Olypiade' (aka 'Rubidor'), Golden Jackpot®, or Sonic Bloom® Ghost®, all of which reach about 1.5 metres and have red flowers. 'Flamingo Pink' has pink flowers and yellow early summer leaves that turn lime green later in the season.

The oldest purple-leaved cultivar is 'Java Red', which reaches 120 centimetres. However, the darker-leaved Wine series are the most popular: Wine and Roses® (120 centimetres), Spilled Wine® (90 centimetres), Fine Wine® (90 centimetres), and Midnight Wine® (30 centimetres). All have purple-pink flowers. 'Dark Horse' has perhaps the darkest foliage and can reach 90 centimetres.

Less commonly seen but worth growing is *F. middendorffianum*, called the yellow weigela as it has straw yellow flowers with a deeper golden yellow throat. It can reach 1.5 metres. All weigela are useful as foundation plants or informal hedging, or in a mixed border. The dwarf cultivars may be used in rockeries. All attract hummingbirds and bumblebees.

Weigela grow best in full sun with reasonably fertile, well-drained but evenly moist soil. They do not tolerate drought. Propagation is by summer or hardwood cuttings. Overall, they are care-free plants with few pests or diseases. *Weigela florida* is hardy to zone 4, while *W. middendorffianum* is rated for zone 5.

Weigela florida Wine and Roses®.

Xanthoceras sorbifolium.

Xanthoceras sorbifolium
YELLOWHORN

Yellowhorn, X*anthoceras sorbifolium*, is an uncommon plant in Atlantic Canada. This Chinese species may grow as a 7-metre-tall tree, but more often is shrubby, reaching 3 metres. Its shiny pinnate leaves, which turn yellow in autumn, look like miniature mountain-ash leaves. They turn yellow in autumn. In June, plants produce masses of white, starlike flowers in terminal narrow clusters. An attractive feature of the flowers is that their centres change from yellow to red as they age. The resulting fruit are globular with large edible black seeds.

These care-free plants need full sun and any well-drained soil. It tolerates some drought once it is established. Pests and diseases are rare. Propagation is by seed. This species is rated hardy to zone 4, but as it appreciates summer heat, it grows better in inland locations.

Yucca
YUCCA, ADAM'S NEEDLE

Yucca are native to North and Central America, where they typically grow in deserts. Only two species tolerate the cold, wet conditions of Atlantic Canada—*Yucca glauca* and *Y. filamentosa*. Both produce 60- to 80-centimetre-high rosettes of evergreen strap- to swordlike leaves. As they have a woody stem, they are technically shrubs, although many gardeners grow them as perennials. *Yucca glauca* has narrower leaves that are often grey- or blue-green. It is not as commonly grown in Atlantic Canada as *Y. filamentosa*. The wild form of *Y. filamentosa* also has blue-green foliage. 'Excalibur' has been selected for its intense steel blue foliage. 'Bright Edge' has leaves narrowly edged in yellow, while 'Colour Guard' and 'Garland Gold' have yellow leaves edged in green. Once mature, these yucca produce, in July or August, a stem up to 2.6 metres tall, topped with a panicle of nodding, white bell-shaped flowers.

Yucca need plenty of sun and a warm site with excellent drainage, particularly in winter. As they grow in dry sites as well as sandy or salty soil,

Yucca filamentosa 'Colour Guard'.

they are wonderful subjects for a coastal garden. No pests or diseases bother them. Propagation is by removal of the many offsets that develop around the parent plant. They are hardy to zone 5, even zone 4 with winter protection. Generally, they do not grow well in Newfoundland, as the climate is too wet with not enough summer heat to keep them healthy.

Yucca filamentosa.

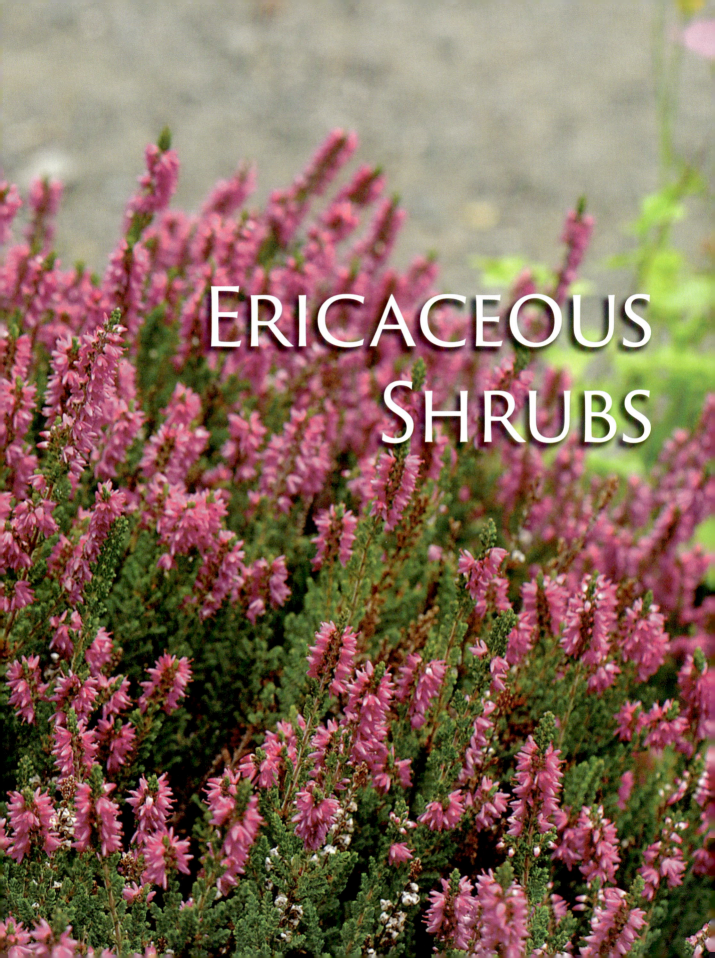

Ericaceous Shrubs

Andromeda polifolia 'Blue Ice'.
LEFT: *Andromeda polifolia* 'Kiri Kaming'.
PREVIOUS SPREAD: *Calluna vulgaris* 'Darkness'.

Andromeda polifolia
BOG ROSEMARY

The single species of *Andromeda*, *A. polifolia*, is a bogland plant found throughout the northern hemisphere. North American populations, formerly called *A. glaucophylla*, are now known as *A. polifolia* var. *glaucophylla*. It is a common plant of peatlands throughout Atlantic Canada. The genus was named by Carl von Linnaeus in 1732 as a tribute to the Greek goddess Andromeda. Bog rosemary is a small 10- to 50-centimetre-tall suckering shrub, with narrow, rugose, evergreen leaves that vary from dark green to grey- to blue-green. It often takes on purple tones in winter. The nodding, urn-shaped, white to pink flowers are borne in loose terminal clusters in May or June. There are several named selections. 'Compacta' is a dwarf form usually less than 15 centimetres. 'Macrophylla' has larger, wider leaves than the standard bog rosemary. 'Kirigamine', often misspelled as 'Kiri-Kaming', is a compact form whose grey-green leaves often have a fine red margin. 'Growler', a selection released by the Memorial University of Newfoundland Botanical Garden, is similar to 'Kirigamine' but has a notable plum purple winter colour. 'Blue Ice', a larger plant reaching 30 centimetres tall, is selected for its consistent blue-green foliage. Derived as a sport from 'Blue Ice' is 'Blue Lagoon', whose foliage is silvery blue.

Bog rosemary, as the name suggests, require sandy-peaty, acidic soil that is consistently moist. Full sun is best to maintain compact plants and prolific blooms. Plants may be lightly trimmed to maintain a rounded habit. Use them as a foliage contrast among heaths, heathers, and dwarf rhododendrons. It is also useful in moist pockets of a rock garden. Bog rosemary is rarely bothered by pests or diseases. Propagation is by fall cuttings. It is super-hardy, rated for zone 2.

Arctostaphylos uva-ursi
BEARBERRY, KINNIKINNIK

Most of the 66 species of *Arctostaphylos* are distributed in the western mountains of the Americas, with one species extending into Eurasia. The genus name *Arctostaphylos* means grapes of the bear, referring to the popularity of the fruit of this genus as an autumn food source for bears. *A. uva-ursi*, native in Atlantic Canada, has trailing stems and forms a dense spreading mat with spoon-shaped evergreen leaves that are often tinted wine red in autumn. The urn-shaped

Arctostaphylos uva-ursi.

Arctostaphylos uva-ursi.

white to pink flowers are produced in terminal clusters in June. In fall, these become bright red berries that often remain on the plant through the winter. 'Massachusetts', the oldest selection, is grown for its abundant flowers and fruit, disease resistance, and slightly more compact habit. 'Vancouver Jade' is similar but stays greener in winter. 'Wood's Red', the densest selection, tolerates more shade than others.

Bearberry perform best in sandy-peaty soil located in full sun to light shade. It is drought-, wind-, and salt-tolerant. Usually it is grown as a ground cover on embankments or under tall trees but it can also be used in rock gardens or cascading over retaining walls. It is particularly well suited to coastal gardens. Pests and diseases are rare, but excessive moisture or heat can lead to a variety of fungal leaf issues. Propagation is by fall cuttings. Bearberry is super-hardy, rated for zone 2.

Calluna vulgaris
Heather

C. vulgaris is the single species within the genus *Calluna*. The genus name comes from the Greek *kalluno*, to clean, a reference to the plant's ancient use as a broom. This species is native across northern Europe to Siberia and is now naturalized in parts of Atlantic Canada. This evergreen shrub has tiny overlapping scalelike leaves arranged in four rows along the wiry stems. The flowers are produced in terminal one-sided racemes from midsummer through fall. Individual flowers are typically purple-pink, bell-shaped, and quite small but together create a pleasing effect. Popular as a garden plant for hundreds of years, over 800 named cultivars are now available. Flowers range from white through every imaginable shade of pink and purple, as well as nearly red. Several, like 'Kinlochruel' (white), 'County Wicklow' (light pink), and 'Radnor' (pink), have fully double miniature pompomlike

Calluna vulgaris.

flowers. Even bud-type heathers, whose flower buds colour up but never open, are often sold as fall pot plants in local florist shops but are perfectly hardy to grow outside. These bud-types remain attractive well into late fall and even into early winter in milder areas: 'Amethyst' (purple-pink), 'Athene' (red), 'Freya' (light pink), and 'Selly' (deep pink). Heathers vary tremendously in their habit. Some heathers have been selected for their foliage colour. Most popular among grey-foliaged types are 'Silver Queen' (lavender) and 'Silver King' (white). 'Arran Gold' (mauve), 'Beoley Gold' (white), and Gold Haze' (white) were selected for their bright yellow foliage. 'Blazeaway' (lavender), 'Red Haze' (lavender), and 'Sir John Carrington' (lilac-pink) have yellow summer foliage that turns reddish orange in winter. Typically, heathers form clumps with

Calluna vulgaris 'Kinlochruel'.

upright stems which reach 60 centimetres, but many of today's cultivars are bushier, often less than 30 centimetres, with 'Claire Carpet' (light pink) and 'White Lawn' completely prostrate and less than 10 centimetres tall.

Heathers require acidic sandy-peaty soil that is well drained but evenly moist. They do not tolerate droughty soil. Full sun is best to maintain the most flowers and best foliar colour. Plants should be trimmed each spring to remove the old flowers and to maintain a bushier habit. They are usually grown in their own dedicated garden, together with heaths and dwarf rhododendrons. Propagation is by late summer to fall cuttings. Heather are not usually bothered by pests and diseases. It is rated hardy to zone 4.

Cassiope
Mountain Bell Heather

As a group, the nine species of *Cassiope* are found in Arctic regions and points farther south atop the highest mountains. Overall, they are considered snow-bed species—plants that grow beneath late-lying snow, where they are mostly

Cassiope lycopodioides 'Beatrice Lilley'.

protected from the freeze-thaw cycle of fall and spring. This can make them challenging to cultivate in Atlantic Canada. Plants are matlike, 10 to 20 centimetres tall, with prostrate stems and evergreen, overlapping, scalelike leaves. The nodding, white, lily-of-the-valley-like flowers, often with contrasting red calyxes, are solitary near the tips of the stems. Blooming is mid- to late spring. Three main species are grown as garden plants: *C. mertensiana* (Alaska to California), *C. lycopodioides* (Alaska, British Columbia, and northern Washington state), and *C. selaginoides* (Himalayas). Named cultivars 'Badenoch', 'Beatrice Lilley', and 'Muirhead' were selected for their freer flowering habit, as many *Cassiope* can be shy bloomers.

Cassiope require similar conditions as heaths and heathers: acidic, sandy-peaty, well-drained soil and full sun. It does not tolerate excess summer heat and performs better along cooler coastlines. It does not tolerate drought. Propagation is by late summer or fall cuttings. Few pests or diseases bother them. While in the wild they may grow in zone 2; in areas with no reliable winter snow-cover, they are best in zone 5 or milder.

Daboecia cantabrica
St. Daboec's Heath

D. cantabrica, the only species within the genus *Daboecia*, is native to coastal rocky cliffs and dry barrens of southwestern Europe. While stems may reach 40 centimetres, they are generally prostrate, with the plants forming a loose mat up to 1 metre or more wide. The small 1-centimetre-long evergreen leaves are glossy green on the topside of the leaf and white on the underside, with inrolled margins. The flowers are produced in loose terminal racemes. Individual flowers are urn-shaped, 10 to 14 millimetres long, and generally shades of reddish purple. Plants have a prolonged blooming period from late June until October. There are over 50 named selections to choose from, which differ in their mature size and floral colour. Among the more popular are 'Atropurpurea' (dark purple), 'Hookstone Purple' (purple), 'Cinderella' (light pink), 'Amelie' (magenta), 'Angelina' (reddish pink), 'Vanessa'

Daboecia cantabrica 'Bicolor'.

(mauve), 'Snowdrift' (white), and 'Alba' (white). Unique is 'Bicolor', whose flowers are either magenta, white, or striped with both colours, all on the same plant. For decorative foliage, try 'Rainbow', whose leaves are flecked with yellow and its flowers are purple-pink.

Daboecia, closely related to heaths and heathers, combine well with them, and require similar growing conditions. The soil should be acidic and highly organic but well drained. Full sun is preferred in cooler regions but part shade in warm, inland areas. A light shearing each spring keep plants tidy. Pests and diseases are rare. Propagation is by late summer to fall cuttings. It is tenderer than heaths and heathers, rated for zone 6, so it is only reliable in the mildest areas of Atlantic Canada.

Enkianthus
REDVEIN ENKIANTHUS

There are about 12 species of *Enkianthus*, all native to eastern Asia. They are large shrubs or small trees with elliptical, finely serrated leaves that are often in whorls. Many have spectacular fall foliage in shades of red and orange. The exquisite, nodding bell-like white to red flowers are produced in terminal clusters in late spring. The most commonly grown species is the Japanese species *E. campanulatus*, which can reach 4 metres tall and has a narrow, upright form. The creamy white flowers have red veins. 'Red Bells' has pink flowers with reddish pink tips, while 'Lipstick' has cream flowers with hot pink tips. 'Showy Lantern' and 'Pagoda' have completely pink flowers. 'Bruce Briggs' has the darkest flow-

Enkianthus campanulatus 'Lipstick'.

Enkianthus campanulatus 'Red Bells'.

Erica vagans 'Valerie Proudley'.

ers of any selection, nearly red. *Enkianthus perulatus* is smaller than *E. campanulatus*, reaching 2 to 3 metres in height, with nearly pure white flowers. The most popular selection is 'J.L. Pennock'. *Enkianthus cernuus* f. *rubens* is also more compact, at 2 metres, but with a rounded habit. Its red bells are held in drooping racemes of up to 12 blossoms. These last two have a much slower growth rate than *E. campanulatus*. *Enkianthus* are usually combined with other taller ericaceous shrubs such as mountain laurels, Japanese andromeda, and rhododendrons.

All *Enkianthus* require acidic, organic-rich soil that is evenly moist but well drained. Full sun produces the most flowers and best fall colour, but part shade is tolerated. Propagation is by summer cuttings or seed. It has no known serious pests or diseases. *Enkianthus campanulatus* is the hardiest, at zone 4. *Enkianthus cernuus* is rated for zone 5; *E. perulatus*, zone 6.

Erica
Heath

Of the hundreds of species of *Erica*, most of them from South Africa, the few that are grown in Atlantic Canada are all natives of Europe. The one common feature is tiny needlelike leaves. They fall into two groups: spring bloomers and summer bloomers. The more popular, spring-blooming heaths start to bloom as soon as the snow melts in April and can continue into early June. They are important nectar plants for early emerging bees and butterflies. *Erica carnea* and *E.* X *darleyensis*, the main spring heaths, form low mounds 15 to 30 centimetres tall. Their narrow urn-shaped flowers are white, red, purple, or various shades of pink. Popular cultivars include 'Darley Dale' (shell pink), 'December Red', 'Heathwood' (lilac-pink), 'King George' (deep pink), 'Pirbright Rose', 'Springwood Pink', 'Springwood White', and 'Vivelli'

Erica carnea.

(magenta). While most have green foliage, a few have colourful foliage that may be yellow, orange, or reddish, adding both summer and winter interest to the ericaceous garden. Some suggested cultivars with coloured foliage are 'Ann Sparkes' (orange-yellow, rose pink flowers), 'Aurea' (yellow, rose pink flowers), 'Golden Starlet' (yellow, white flowers), and 'Jack H. Brummage' (orange-yellow, heliotrope flowers).

Among the summer-blooming heaths, the most commonly seen are *E. tetralix*, *E. cinerea*, and *E. vagans*. *Erica tetralix*, or cross heath, has grey-green, pubescent leaves and terminal clusters of nodding flowers from July through frost. Among the most popular cultivars are 'Alba Mollis' (white), 'Con Underwood' (magenta), and 'Pink Star' (lilac-pink). *Erica cinerea*, or bell heather, also has terminal clusters of flowers, but the foliage is dark green. Suggested cultivars are 'Cindy' (purple), 'Eden Valley' (lavender), 'Golden Hue'

Erica tetralix 'Alba Mollis'.

Erica cineria 'Atropurpurea'.

(yellow foliage, amethyst flowers), 'Pink Ice' (rose pink), and 'Velvet Night' (dark purple-red). Cornish heath, *E. vagans*, has masses of tiny flowers nestled among the leaf axils along the branch tips. The most popular is probably 'Mrs. D. F. Maxwell' (deep rose pink), but also consider 'Kevernensis Alba' (white), 'Pyrenees Pink' and 'St. Keverne' (pink). Hybrid summer-blooming heaths include *E.* X *watsonii* 'Dawn' (deep pink), *E.* X *stuartii* 'Irish Lemon' (yellow foliage, mauve flowers), and *E.* X *griffithsii* 'Jacqueline' (fragrant cherry red flowers). As with heathers, these are just a sampling of the many hundreds of heath cultivars available.

Heaths require organic-rich, well-drained soil and a position in full sun. They are often combined with heathers and dwarf rhododendrons, but the spring-blooming heaths are also wonderful when mixed with spring-flowering bulbs. Pests and disease are uncommon but hares may nibble the stems. Propagation is by late summer to fall cuttings. Most are hardy through zone 5, except *E.* X *griffithsii*, which is rated for zone 6.

Gaultheria
WINTERGREEN

About 135 species of *Gaultheria* are found throughout North and South America, Asia, Australia, and New Zealand. The South American species were once placed in their own genus, *Pernettya*, but today are included in *Gaultheria*. *Pernettya mucronata* is so well known under its original name that it is included in this book under that name. The genus *Gaultheria* honours Jean-Francois Gaulthier, a Quebec physician and naturalist of the mid-1700s. As a group, the wintergreens are broad-leaved evergreens with nodding urn-shaped white to deep pink flowers which are either solitary or produced in clusters. Flowers develop into fleshy berries which vary from white, pink, purple, blue, or black, some of which are edible. The plant sizes vary from a few centimetres to over 5 metres tall. Only a few are hardy and of ornamental value as garden subjects. Perhaps the most recognized by Maritime gardeners is our native American wintergreen or teaberry, *G. procumbens*. It is a low 10- to 15-centimetre-tall shrub with stiff, glossy deep green foliage that is red-tinted in the spring, green in summer, and becomes red-tinted again in winter. Flowering commences in midsummer, with edible red berries developed in late autumn. These berries often remain attached for up to a

Gaultheria miquelliana.

Gaultheria procumbens.

Kalmia
MOUNTAIN LAUREL, BOG LAUREL

All eight species of *Kalmia* are native to North America. The genus name honours Swedish botanist Peter Kalm (1716–1779), who botanized in parts of eastern North America from 1747 to 1751. While all have some merit as garden plants, only one species has been widely cultivated as a garden ornamental, *K. latifolia*, the mountain laurel. This medium-to-tall shrub, 3 to 9 metres tall, is native primarily along the Appalachian Mountains. Plants have lance-shaped, dark green, glossy, evergreen foliage. Terminal clusters of saucer-shaped, 2.5-centimetre-diameter, white to pink flowers are produced in early summer to midsummer. The gnarled stems of older plants add charm to any garden. Many named selections have been developed, most of which generally remain less than 2.5 metres

year. It is commonly seen as an understory plant of open forests. Salal, *G. shallon*, is native from Alaska south to California, where it grows as an understory plant of coniferous forests. A suckering shrub, it reaches 2 metres, with stiff, leathery, egg-shaped leaves which are popular for floral arrangements. The clustered flowers, produced in late spring, become dark blue edible berries in autumn.

From northern Japan, Sakhalin Island, and the Aleutian Islands comes Miquel's wintergreen, *G. miqueliana*. This suckering shrub reaches 20 to 30 centimetres tall and has oval, matte green, distinctly veined leaves. Clusters of white flowers are often hidden under the leaves but develop into large, decorative white berries in late summer and fall.

All *Gaultheria* require humus-rich, acidic soil that does not dry out. Dappled shade is best, but if the soil stays reasonably moist, they tolerate full sun. Deep shade is also tolerated but fewer flowers or fruit will result. Wintergreen are often grown as woodland plants or naturalized under trees. Miquel's wintergreen is best to grow as a ground cover. Pests are not generally a problem, but anthracnose and mildew can be problematic in certain regions. Propagation is by division, summer to fall cuttings, or seed. American wintergreen is hardy to zone 3; Miquel's wintergreen, zone 5; and salal, zone 6.

Kalmia latifolia 'Freckles'.
NEXT PAGE: *Kalmia latifolia* 'Carousel'.

tall. Popular pink cultivars are 'Bridesmaid', 'Heart of Fire', 'Olympic Fire', 'Ostbo Red', 'Sarah', and 'Raspberry Glow'. 'Silver Dollar' and 'Snowdrift' have pure white flowers; 'Mitternacht', 'Kaleidoscope', and 'Keepsake' have dark wine red blossoms. 'Freckles', 'Olympic Wedding', 'Moyland', and 'Pinwheel' have pink and red bicoloured flowers; 'Bullseye', 'Minuet', and 'Peppermint' have two-tone white and wine flowers. 'Madeline' is noteworthy for having double pale pink flowers. The dwarf cultivars have smaller leaves on plants about 1 metre tall. These include 'Elf' (nearly white), 'Firecracker' (light pink), 'Little Linda' (pink), 'Tiddlywink' (pale pink), and 'Tinkerbell' (medium pink). Mountain laurel are ideal companions for rhododendrons, since they flower just after the main rhododendron season.

Less commonly seen as a garden ornamental, but nonetheless noteworthy, is the bog laurel, *K. polifolia*, found across much of Canada and the northeastern US. It is a low, open shrub, less than 1 metre in height, with narrow, dark green, glossy foliage and terminal clusters of pink flowers in late spring. 'Leucantha' is a particularly attractive white form.

Mountain laurel require cool, moist, acidic yet well-drained soil. Mountain laurel and rhododendrons thrive in the same type of soil. A peaty-sandy loam is perfect. Clay soil should be avoided. The ideal light is dappled shade or, at the least, shade from hot afternoon sun. Bog laurel, on the other hand, demand full sun and peaty, consistently moist if not wet, conditions. Little pruning is required for either, except dead-heading. Pests and diseases are rare. All parts of the plant are toxic if ingested by humans. Propagation is by fall cuttings. Mountain laurel is best grown in zone 5 or warmer but has been known to survive in sheltered areas of zone 4. Bog laurel is hardy to zone 2.

TODD BOLAND

Leiophyllum buxifolium
SAND-MYRTLE

As of 2008, *Leiophyllum* were reclassified as *Kalmia* but is described here by its more familiar name. The single species, *L. buxifolium* (now *K. buxifolia*), is restricted to three locations in eastern US: the New Jersey Pine Barrens, the coastal plain of the Carolinas, and the southeastern Blue Ridge Mountains. Sand-myrtle is a low broad-leaved evergreen shrub, generally less than 30 centimetres high. The round to elliptical leaves are about 1 centimetre long. Summer foliage is glossy green, taking on bronzy tones in winter. In late spring, plants produce terminal, rounded clusters of small starlike white or pink-tinted flowers. There are several cultivars: 'Prostratum', with trailing stems; 'Pinecake', which has a dwarf mounding habit; and 'Eco Red Stem', which has distinctive red stems. Sand-myrtle are usually grown among heaths and heathers but may also be used in rock gardens.

Sand-myrtle require full sun to part shade and peaty-sandy acidic soil that retains some moisture yet is well drained. Propagation is by summer cuttings. It has no serious pests or diseases and is rated hardy to zone 5.

Leiophyllum buxifolium.

Leucothöe
Drooping leucothöe, fetterbush

About 50 species of leucothöe, distributed primarily in North America and Asia, are deciduous or broad-leaved evergreen shrubs 1 to 3 metres tall, with lance-shaped leaves and axillary drooping clusters of white urn-shaped flowers in late May through June. Those that are commonly grown as garden ornamentals in temperate areas are the broad-leaved evergreen types. Perhaps the most well recognized species is *L. fontanesiana*, native to the Appalachians. This species can reach 2 metres tall but is more commonly low and spreading to 1 metre. *Leucothöe axillaris* is similar, but in the wild grows closer to the coast rather than in the mountains. There are several selections of both *Leucothöe* species and possibly hybrids too. Scarletta® has bright red spring leaves that later turn glossy green only to take on red and burgundy tones again in winter. 'Rainbow', aka 'Girard's Rainbow', has leaves that are irregularly streaked with cream and yellow. For those with small gardens, try 'Compacta', which is dense and bushy, reaching 1 metre tall, or 'Nana', which grows 30 to 60 centimetres high. Both have good red to burgundy winter colour. Leafscape™ 'Little Flames' is a dwarf culti-

Leucothöe davisiae.

var whose spring leaves are red, winter leaves are wine, and in summer, retain red-tipped leaves, looking, as the name suggests, like flickering candles. Red Lips® is similar but retains burgundy colour all year long. Curly Red® is similar but has smaller, distinctly curled foliage. These last three dwarf cultivars rarely produce flowers. From northern California and Oregon comes *L. davisiae*, a suckering shrub 30 to 60 centimetres tall with glossy bright green foliage and erect racemes of white flowers in early summer.

The most popular Asian species, *L. keiskei*, is similar to a compact form of *L. axillaris*. Named cultivars include 'Halloween', 'Royal Ruby', and Burning Love®, all bushy 30- to 60-centimetre-tall shrubs with red spring growth and dark green summer leaves, which become wine-tinted

Leucothöe fontanesiana 'Nana'.

in winter. 'Halloween' is noted for its very narrow foliage. These cultivars are grown primarily for their foliage, as flowers are scarce.

Most *Leucothöe* require evenly moist, acidic, humus-rich soil; *Leucothöe davisiae* is an exception, as it tolerates reasonably dry soil. Dappled shade is ideal, but if kept moist, they tolerate full sun. Deep shade is also tolerated, but flower production and attractive leaf colour are reduced. Propagation is by fall cuttings. These care-free plants are not susceptible to pests and diseases, with the possible exception of leaf spotting, if the location is too sheltered. The above are hardy to zone 6, and even zone 5, if provided protection from winter winds.

Pernettya mucronata
PRICKLY HEATH

The single species of *Pernettya* that sometimes appears in local gardens, *P. mucronata*, is native to the Andes of Chile and Argentina. Botanically, this plant is now known as *Gaultheria mucronata*, but since it is so well known in the literature as *Pernettya*, it is described in this book under that name. This 45- to 120-centimetre-tall evergreen shrub has small, shiny, spiny-tipped leaves not unlike those of a miniature holly. And like holly, these plants are dioecious. Both male and female plants produce small, white, urn-shaped flowers in late spring or early summer. In autumn, female plants, if pollinated, produce decorative pearl-like berries in shades of pink, red, magenta, or white. These fruit often remain through much of the winter. One male plant can pollinate several females. Named cultivars include 'Snow White' (white berries), 'Mulberry Wine' (magenta-purple fruit), 'Crimsonia' (crimson fruit), and 'Pink Pearl' (light pink fruit).

Pernettya require evenly moist, acidic, humus-rich soil in full sun or part shade. It tolerates

Pernettya mucronata.

boggy soil. Plants may be trimmed to keep them dense and compact. While diseases are rare, hares relish the foliage. Propagation is by fall cuttings. *Pernettya* is borderline hardy in Atlantic Canada. Plants are most successful in southernmost Nova Scotia, but if well protected in winter, *Pernettya* can survive milder areas of zone 5.

Pernettya mucronata.

Phyllodoce
MOUNTAIN HEATHER

All eight species of *Phyllodoce*, a genus named for a sea nymph of Greek mythology, are confined to the Arctic regions of the northern hemisphere, with some extending south along higher mountain ranges. In their native haunts, they are considered snow-bed species, growing where late-lying snow does not expose them to fluctuating freeze-thaw. As a result, many are challenging to cultivate. They are low-growing shrubs, rarely exceeding 30 centimetres tall. Their leaves are needlelike and much like a larger version of spring heath, *Erica carnea*. The flowers are terminal, either solitary or in clusters, blooming in early summer. Individual flowers are urn- to bell-shaped, nodding, and either creamy white or purple-pink. Perhaps the easiest in cultivation is *P. glanduliflora*, which has clusters of cream-white flowers that are covered in sticky hairs. In the wild, it is native to subalpine and alpine habitats from Alaska south to Wyoming. With a similar range is *P. empetriformis*, whose purple-pink flowers are in clusters. A hybrid between these two is *P.* X *intermedia* 'Fred Stoker', which has light pink urn-shaped flowers.

Phyllodoce need similar soil conditions as heaths and heathers: moist, acidic, and sandy-peaty with good drainage and full sun. Propagation is by late summer to fall cuttings. Pests or disease are rare. Plants are hardy to zone 3; however, they do not grow well in summer heat and perform best along cooler coastlines.

Pieris
ANDROMEDA

The seven species of *Pieris* are native to East Asia or North America. All are broad-leaved evergreens with glossy foliage and terminal clusters of nodding, white, urn-shaped fragrant flowers. Two species of *Pieris* are grown in Atlantic Canada as garden ornamentals—Japanese andromeda, *P. japonica*, and to a lesser degree, mountain andromeda, *P. floribunda*. The latter, native to the mountains of southeastern US, can reach 2 me-

Phyllodoce glanduliflora.

Pieris japonica.

Pieris japonica.

Pieris 'Brouwer's Beauty'.

tres in height, with elliptical leaves. The flower stems are erect and the newly emerging leaves are yellow-green, both features that separate it from the similar Japanese andromeda, whose flower stems are arching and newly emerging leaves are red or at least red-tinted. Mountain andromeda blooms from April to May. The only cultivar is 'Millstream', which is compact, bushy, and generally less than 1 metre tall. Japanese andromeda is native to eastern China, Taiwan, and Japan. Similar to mountain andromeda, it can reach 4 metres. It also blooms from April through May. This species has many named cultivars. 'Forest Flame', 'Mountain Fire', and 'Bonfire' are cultivars with particularly striking bright red spring foliage. Larger cultivars with white-edged foliage are 'Flaming Silver', 'White Rim', 'Carnaval', and 'Fire N Ice'. Among those dwarf cultivars less than 1 metre tall are 'Cavatine', 'Debutante', 'Little Heath Green', and 'Prelude'. 'Little Heath' is a dwarf cultivar with variegated foliage. A few cultivars have pink flowers, rather than the standard white: 'Cabernet', 'Valley Rose', 'Valley Valentine', and Passion Party™. Enchanted Forest™ Impish Elf® is a dwarf pink-flowered selection. Perhaps the most striking is Passion Party™ Passion Frost™, which has both variegated leaves and cherry pink flowers. 'Brouwer's Beauty' is a hybrid between mountain and Japanese andromeda whose spring leaves are yellow-green like those of mountain andromeda but the flowers are on arching stems.

Pieris require acidic, well-drained, humus-rich soil in full sun or part shade. It does not tolerate poorly drained sites. Propagation is by fall cuttings. As all parts of *Pieris* are toxic if ingested, they are not bothered by larger herbivores. The main disease is root rot, especially if drainage is poor. Both species have brittle stems that can be damaged by heavy, wet snow loads. Mountain andromeda is hardy to zone 4; 'Brouwer's Beauty', zone 5. Japanese andromeda is reliably hardy to zone 6 but worth trying in sheltered areas of zone 5.

Pieris japonica 'Mountain Fire'.

Rhododendron
RHODODENDRON

Over 1,000 species of *Rhododendron*, plus thousands of hybrids, are considered *the* most important group of ornamental flowering shrubs. The description here does not do justice to the wonderful array of variety and flower colour that exists in this genus. For simplicity, rhododendrons are broken into five groups: Vireya rhododendrons of the tropics (beyond the focus of this book); large-leaved evergreen rhododendrons of the Elepidote group; small-leaved evergreen rhododendrons of the Lepidote group; evergreen azaleas; and deciduous azaleas. The azaleas will be described separately.

The classical large-leaved, large-trussed rhododendrons are what rhododendron taxonomists call the Elepidotes. In Atlantic Canada, such rhododendrons are typically 1 to 4 metres

Rhododendron dauricum 'Album'.
PREVIOUS SPREAD: *Rhododendron* border.

Rhododendron 'Blue Baron'.

152   SHRUBS AND VINES FOR ATLANTIC CANADA

tall, growing as wide-spreading shrubs. The hardiest of these are the old-fashioned Catawba or Ironclad hybrids such as 'Grandiflorum' (lavender), 'English Roseum' (pink), 'Boursault' (rose-lavender), 'Roseum Elegans' (lilac), 'Nova Zembla' (cherry red), and 'Catawbiense Album' (white). More recently, many hardy hybrids have been developed in Finland. These are generally shorter plants, 1 to 2 metres tall. The hybrids include 'Baden Baden' (dwarf, red), 'Haaga' (pink), 'Hellikki' (violet-red), 'Helsinki University' (deep pink), 'Mikkeli' (white), 'Raisa' (dwarf, purple), and 'Pohjola's Daughter' (light pink). The Yak hybrids, developed from *R. yakushimanum*, have the bonus of new leaves covered in silvery white to fawn-coloured feltlike indumentum. This wears away during the summer but is retained on the undersurface of the leaves. These typically have flowers that open pink and fade to white. Popular among these are 'Mist Maiden', 'Ken Janeck', 'Crete', 'Yaku Prince', and 'Yaku Princess'. Many other hardy elepidote rhododendrons are available, in shades of pink, purple, red, and yellow, along with white and bicoloured. Check with a local nursery for their latest offerings.

The lepidote rhododendrons typically have smaller leaves and flowers. Some bloom earlier than the elepidotes; others flower at the same time. Many are very dwarf, making them suitable for rock gardens or an ericaceous border, where they may be mixed with heaths and heathers. Others are tall, reaching 3 metres or more. They are sometime erroneously called azaleas (see next page). Among the taller lepidotes are the PJM series. Many of these have leaves that turn bronzy to deep purple in winter. They flower quite early, late April to mid-May, with small

Rhododendron 'PJM'.

rounded trusses of purple to reddish pink flowers. Popular hybrids include 'Aglo' (bright pink), 'April Dawn' (pale pink), 'Bubblegum' (lipstick pink), 'Checkmate' (lavender-pink), 'Midnight Ruby' (pink, dark purple winter foliage), 'Olga' (lavender-pink), and 'PJ Mezitt' (lavender purple). Double-flowered hybrids also exist: 'April Rose' (purple-pink) and 'April Mist' (light pink). Taller and very early blooming are also the *R. dauricum/mucronulatum* selections. These reach 2 metres or more and are semi-deciduous, losing many of their leaves over the winter. 'Madison Snow' and 'Cornell Pink' are the most popular.

Plenty of low-stature lepidotes less than 30 centimetres tall are available: 'Ginny Gee' (two-tone pink), 'Patty Bee' (yellow), 'Purple Gem' (purple), 'Ramapo' (purple), and *R. impeditum* (purple-blue).

Rhododendrons need full sun to part shade and acidic, organic-rich but well-drained soil. They do not tolerate drought, soggy soil, or salt. As they retain their leaves all winter, they need to be positioned in a sheltered location; otherwise, they risk significant winter burn. Few pests or diseases bother them in Atlantic Canada, except root rot, which can occasionally occur, and root weevils, which cause scalloped leaf edges. Propagation is by fall cuttings. The Ironclads, Finnish Yak, and PJM hybrids are hardy to zone 4; the others, zones 5 or 6.

Rhododendron
AZALEA

Two groups of rhododendrons are commonly called azaleas. The first group are broad-leaved evergreens. Many gardeners are familiar with florist azaleas, commonly sold in nurseries and box stores between Valentine's Day and Mother's Day. These azaleas are not hardy in Atlantic Canada. However, several similar azaleas will

Rhododendron 'White Lights'.

survive in the milder areas of Atlantic Canada. These are either evergreen or semi-evergreen. The hardiest are *R. yedoense*, *R. poukhanense*, *R. obtusum*, *R. kaempferi*, and their hybrids. The species are not easy to find but hybrids to look for include the various Girard hybrids (mixed shades of pink, purple, red, or white), 'Stewartsonian' (orange-red), and 'Elsie Lee' (pink). Most of these are low growing, less than 1 metre tall, but wide-spreading. They bloom mostly in June.

Far hardier are the deciduous azaleas. These

Rhododendron luteum.

vary in height from less than 45 centimetres to over 3 metres. Some bloom as early as May or as late as July, but June is the peak season. Deciduous azaleas have larger trusses than the evergreen types, are fragrant, and come in a wider range of colours, including bright yellow and orange. They have the bonus of excellent fall colour in shades of orange and red. Royal azalea, *R. schlippenbachii*, and pinkshell azalea, *R. vaseyi*, are the earliest to bloom, flowering in May-early June before they flush leaves. Originating from Europe are the Gent, Knaphill, and Exbury hybrids. These older hybrids are still widely available. Suggested hybrids include 'Klondyke' (golden yellow), 'Gibralter' (orange), 'Fireball' (orange-red), 'Mount Saint Helens' (pink), 'Cannon's Double' (pink and yellow, double-flowered), and 'Oxydol' (white). The hardiest are the Northern Lights series, which are available in a wide range of colours. The hybrids all have the name 'Lights' in their name, such as 'Manda-

Rhododendron 'Rosy Lights'.

rin Lights' and 'Orchid Lights'. To extend the blooming season of azaleas, try the Weston hybrids. These are generally dwarf, about 1 metre tall, and bloom very late, well into July or even August.

Like rhododendrons, azaleas need acidic, organic-rich, well-drained but evenly moist soil. Full sun results in the most blooms, but evergreen azaleas tolerate some shade. Pests are not common, but powdery mildew can occur if the site is too sheltered. Propagation is by summer cuttings. Deciduous azaleas are mostly hardy to zone 5, with the Northern Lights series rated for zone 4. Evergreen azaleas are most reliable in zone 6 but, with good winter protection, have been known to survive in zone 5.

X *Phylliopsis hillieri*

Intergeneric plant crosses (hybrids between two different genera) are rare outside the world of orchids. Among the Ericaceae, the only intergeneric hybrid likely to be encountered as a garden ornamental is X *Phylliopsis*, a cross between *Phyllodoce* and *Kalmiopsis*. While both genera are challenging to grow in gardens, the hybrid is actually more amenable. This hybrid resembles the

X *Phylliopsis* 'Sugar Plum'.

X *Phylliopsis* 'Pinocchio'.

Phyllodoce parent: a low mound 15 to 30 centimetres high, with narrow, almost needlelike leaves. The flowers, produced in terminal racemes in early summer, may be urn-shaped or open and bell-shaped, but always a shade of purple-pink. There are three main hybrids: 'Coppelia', which is *P. emptriformis* X *K. leachiana*; 'Sugar Plum', which is *P. caerulea* X *K. leachiana*; and 'Pinocchio', which is *P. breweri* X *K. leachiana*.

Like most ericaceae, X *Phylliopsis* require acidic, sandy-peaty soil that is evenly moist but well drained. Full sun is preferred. Propagation is by late summer to fall cuttings. Pests and diseases are rare. They are rated hardy to zone 4 but dislike excess summer heat; they are best grown in cooler coastal areas.

Zenobia pulverulenta.

Zenobia pulverulenta
Honey-cup, Dusty Zenobia

The single species of *Zenobia*, *Z. pulverulenta*, is a suckering, twiggy shrub 1 to 3 metres tall, native to the southeast US. The leathery elliptical to oval leaves may be up to 10 centimetres long. The summer foliage is often covered in a dusty grey- to blue-green waxy bloom. In fall, the foliage turns reddish purple, especially if grown in full sun. In mild areas, plants are semi-evergreen but at the northern end of their range, they are deciduous. From June to July, plants produce bell-shaped, lily-of-the-valley-like white flowers in nodding axillary clusters. The flowers have a strong anise fragrance. Both 'Blue Sky' and 'Woodlander's Blue' are selections chosen for their intense blue-grey foliage. 'Raspberry Ripple' has typical grey-green foliage but its claim to fame is its deep pink-edged flowers.

Zenobia may be grown in full sun to part shade, in moist, sandy-peaty soil. Pests and diseases are generally not a problem, but as the stems are weak, they may be damaged under heavy snow loads. Propagation is by summer cuttings or seed. As it is rated hardy to zone 6, it is only suitable for the mildest areas of Atlantic Canada.

Conifers

Abies koreana 'Kohout's Icebreaker'.
LEFT: *Abies balsamea* 'Nana'.
PREVIOUS SPREAD: *Microbiota decussata*.

Abies
FIR

Although 50 species of *Abies* have been named, relatively few dwarf shrubby forms are available in Atlantic Canada. The most common is probably dwarf balsam fir, *Abies balsamea* 'Nana', which forms an irregular mound up to 60 centimetres tall. 'Piccalo' is similar and more compact. One of the loveliest firs is Korean fir, *A. koreana*. Some Korean fir have twisted needles that show off their white undersides. Compact selections include 'Silberperle' (45 centimetres, silvery needles), 'Blue Eskimo' (30 centimetres, blue-green needles), and 'Cis' (1.5 metres, blue-tinted needles). Other noteworthy dwarf firs are *A. nordmanniana* 'Golden Spreader' (1.5 metres, golden needles), *A. nordmanniana* 'Broom H' (45 centimetres, nestlike, green), *A. procera* 'Glauca Prostrata' (90 centimetres, blue needles), *A. lasiocarpa* 'Green Globe' (1.5 metres, blue-tinted needles), and *A. fraseri* 'Klein's Nest' (90 centimetres, blue-tinted needles). All of these dwarf firs may be used in rock gardens, as specimens, along foundations, or mixed with other conifers, heaths, and heathers.

Firs like full sun and organic-rich, evenly moist soil that is slightly acidic. They do not tolerate wet soil or drought. The main pests are woolly adelgids, spruce budworm, and aphids. Needle rust and twig blight are sometimes a problem. Propagation is by grafting or fall cuttings. *Abies balsamea* is hardy to zone 3; *A. koreana*, zone 4; *A. nordmanniana* and *A. procera*, zone 5.

Chamaecyparis
FALSE CYPRESS

While only six species of *Chamaecyparis* are found worldwide—three from Asia and three from North America—literally hundreds of dwarf cultivars have been developed by the landscape industry. The following descriptions are but the tip of the iceberg. Hinoki cypress, *C. obtusa*, can reach 25 metres or taller, yet has numerous dwarf cultivars. Many of these are characterized by fan-shaped branchlets. Cultivars that have an irregular, broadly pyramidal habit less than 3 metres tall are 'Chabo Yadori' (fluffy growth combined with fanlike spray), 'Coralliformis' (narrow twisted growths reminiscent of

Chamaecyparis pisifera 'Sungold'.

TODD BOLAND

Chamaecyparis obtusa 'Kosteri'.

coral), 'Lemon Twist' (yellow version of 'Coralliformis'), 'Fernspray Gold' (bright yellow, fernlike growth), 'Gemstone' (narrow pyramidal, tight fanlike growth), 'Kosteri' (conical habit; dark green, fanlike growth), 'Nana Gracilis' (conical habit, fanlike growth), 'Nana Lutea' (bright yellow, fanlike growth), 'Torulosa' (twisted branchlets), and 'Tempelhof' (conical habit, fluffy growth). Other dwarf forms have a more globular habit and are often less than 1 metre tall. Examples include 'Pygmaea', 'Butter Ball', and 'Mariesii', the latter with cream-tipped growth.

Sawara cypress, *C. pisifera*, also has many dwarf forms, both upright and broadly pyramidal. The foliage is either droopy and threadlike or soft and feathery. Those with threadlike foliage often have the name 'Filifera' attached to them: 'Filifera Nana' (green), 'Filifera Aurea' (yellow), 'Filifera Aureovariegata' (splashes of creamy yellow), and 'Filifera Sungold' (yellow). 'Golden Mops' is a popular cultivar. All of these forms mound to about 1 metre tall. 'Lemon Thread' is also yellow, with threadlike growth, but is more broadly pyramidal to 2 metres. Those with more feathery growth often have the added name 'Squarrosa': 'Squarrosa Intermedia' (blue-tinted broad pyramid, 2 metres), or 'Squarrosa Minima' (blue globe, 1 metre). Other dwarf forms include 'Baby Blue' (pyramidal, 2 metres), 'Dwarf Blue' (globular, 1.5 metres), and 'Mikko' (globular, 1.5 metres, white-tipped foliage). Very dwarf globular forms about 50 centimetres tall with mosslike growth include 'Golden Pincushion' (yellow), 'Gold Dust' (splashes of yellow), and 'Mini Variegata' (splashes of white).

From California, the impressive Lawson's cypress, *C. lawsoniana*, can be huge, but a limited number of dwarf 1-metre globular forms are available: 'Ellwood's Nymph' (grey-green), 'Golden Nymph', 'Green Globe', and 'Treasure Island' (yellow). From eastern North America is white cypress, *C. thyoides*. The only dwarf cultivars likely to be found in Atlantic Canada are 'Heatherbun' (globular, blue-green turning purplish in winter), 'Andelyensis' (dark green, nearly columnar, 2 metres), and the similar but smaller 'Little Jamie'.

False cypress perform best with full sun and fertile, well-drained soil. It does not tolerate wet or dry sites. As the foliage is easily burned by winter winds, a sheltered location is suggested. Overall, it is not bothered by pests or diseases. Propagation is by fall cuttings. Sawara cypress is the hardiest, suitable for as cold as zone 4. Hinoki and white cypress are rated for zone 5; Lawson's cypress is hardy only to zone 6.

Chamaecyparis pisifera 'Dwarf Blue'.

Cryptomeria japonica 'Vilmoriniana'.

Cryptomeria
JAPANESE CEDAR

The single species of *Cryptomeria*, *C. japonica*, commonly called the Japanese cedar, can reach 20 metres tall but is rarely offered in the nursery industry. The dwarf forms, however, are more regularly seen. These form tight mounds or globes, less than 60 centimetres tall, with prickly olive green needles. Most take on coppery tones in winter. Suggested cultivars include 'Compressa', 'Vilmoriniana', and 'Tenzan'. 'Vilmorin Gold' has the bonus of yellow tips in the spring as new growth commences. These are all wonderful plants for a rock garden, alpine troughs, containers, and bonsai.

Japanese cedar require full sun and evenly moist, organic-rich soil that is on the acidic side. As it is not drought-tolerant and can be burned by winter winds, it is best to provide a sheltered site. This care-free plant has no serious pests or diseases. Propagation is by fall cuttings. It is rated hardy to zone 5.

Juniperus
JUNIPER

Countless cultivars of juniper are small enough to be considered shrubs. In fact, there are more shrubby than treelike types. All cultivars of Atlantic Canada's native creeping juniper, *J. horizontalis*, are shrubs with scalelike needles. The most popular have trailing stems and a ground-cover habit. Grown for their steel blue foliage are 'Bar Harbor', 'Blue Chip', 'Blue

Cryptomeria japonica 'Tenzan'.

Juniperus communis 'Gold Cone'.

Juniperus squamata 'Loderi'.

Prince', Icee Blue®, 'Wiltonii' (aka 'Blue Rug'), 'Hughes', and 'Yukon Belle'. 'Prince of Wales' and 'Plumosa Compacta' have bright green foliage, while 'Mother Lode' has yellow foliage. The other native juniper, common juniper, *J. communis*, has a low spreading habit and sharp olive green needles with white undersides. Popular cultivars are 'Banff', 'Effusa', 'Green Carpet', 'Repanda', Blueberry Delight™, and 'Depressa Aurea', the latter with yellow foliage. Other, upright columnar to narrow pyramidal forms which generally stay less than 2 metres tall are 'Compressa', 'Pencil Point', 'Suecica', and the yellow-foliaged 'Gold Cone'. Singleseed juniper, *J. squamata*, is also generally low and spreading, with sharp needles. 'Blue Star' and 'Blue Carpet' have outstanding steel blue foliage, while 'Dream Joy' and 'Holger' have yellow new growth. 'Golden Dream' has a unique mix of blue and yellow foliage. With blue-green foliage

Juniperus communis 'Depressa Aurea'.

and upright habit is 'Loderi', which may reach 2 metres in height. Extremely popular for bonsai purposes is Japanese juniper, *J. prostrata* 'Nana', which has trailing stems and blue-green foliage. Shore juniper, *J. conferta*, also has trailing stems and sharp, blue-tinted needles. Popular cultivars include 'Blue Pacific' and 'Emerald Sea'.

Rocky mountain juniper, *J. scopulorum*, is a tree reaching 9 to 12 metres tall, typically with scalelike grey-blue needles. Smaller upright forms that reach 3 to 5 metres include 'Witchita Blue', 'Medora', and 'Blue Arrow'. The only low spreading cultivar likely to be encountered is Blue Creeper™. Savin juniper, *J. sabina*, naturally has a spreading habit 1 to 2 metres tall. The most popular cultivars are 'Buffalo', 'Calgary Carpet', 'Arcadia', 'Blue Danube', 'Skandia', 'Moor-Dense', and 'Tamariscifolia New Blue' (aka 'New Blue Tam'). Eastern red cedar, *J. virginiana*, is a tree over 15 metres tall. 'Skyrocket' is a popular narrow pyramidal form which reaches 4 metres, while 'Hetzii' is a 2-metre spreading form with blue foliage and 'Grey Owl' is 1 metre tall, spreading, with grey-green foliage. The wild form of Chinese juniper, *J. chinensis*, is also a tall tree, but many smaller forms, both uprights and wide-spreading, are available. Popular uprights are 'Blaauw', 'Spartan', and 'Angelica Blue'. Perhaps more popular are the spreading yellow-foliaged cultivars: 'Pfitzeriana Aurea', 'Sea of Gold', 'Gold Coast', 'Gold Lace', 'Old Gold', and Gold Star®. Green spreading cultivars include 'Pfitzeraiana', 'Shimpaku', 'San Jose', and 'Mint Julep'. 'Blue Alps' has blue foliage and a spreading habit, while 'Daub's Frosted' has light chartreuse new foliage turning blue-green when mature.

The dwarf upright junipers are popular as foundation plants or used as a formal, living screen. The spreading types are also popular as foundation plants. The creeping types are useful for embankments, rock gardens, or cascading over retaining walls.

Junipers need full sun and well-drained soil. They are drought-tolerant and, in the case of *J. horizontalis* and *J. conferta*, salt-tolerant as well. Junipers are rarely bothered by insects but diseases may be problematic, especially juniper tip blight, root rot, and apple-cedar rust. Propagation is by fall cuttings. *Juniperus communis*, *J. sabina*, *J. virginiana*, and *J. horizontalis* are rated for zone 3; *J. chinensis*, zone 4; and *J. conferta*, *J. procumbens*, and *J. squamata*, zone 5.

Larix
LARCH

Ten species of *Larix* are found across the northern hemisphere. This conifer is unique in that it is deciduous and loses its needles each fall. The soft needles are bright green to blue-tinted, turning golden yellow in autumn. Only a few dwarf cultivars are available, and these may be chal-

lenging to find, but well worth the effort. *Larix laricina* 'Deborah Waxman', a dwarf 120-centimetre-tall pyramidal version of the native eastern larch, has lovely blue-tinted foliage. Dwarf forms of European larch, *L. decidua*, include 'Prag' and 'Little Bogle', both of which have an irregular globular habit. Japanese larch, *L. kaempferi*, has two notable dwarf forms, 'Wolterdingen' and 'Blue Dwarf', both with blue-tinted needles and irregular globular outlines. Any of the four listed dwarf forms make wonderful subjects for rock gardens.

Larch grow just about anywhere as long as the soil is reasonably good quality and fairly moist, and the site is situated in full sun; they do not tolerate drought. Aphids and sawfly are the main pests, but diseases are rare. Propagation is by summer cuttings or grafting. As all the above are hardy to zone 3, they may be grown throughout Atlantic Canada.

Microbiota decussata
SIBERIAN CYPRESS

Microbiota decussata, a native of Siberia, is the only species within this genus. Superficially, the plant looks like a creeping Chinese juniper without the blue berrylike cones. It grows only to 60 centimetres tall but can spread several metres, making it one of the best ground covers for slopes and embankments. It is particularly attractive cascading over retaining walls. The scalelike foliage is arranged in flat fans and appears almost feathery from a distance. Summer foliage is bright green, but plants turn brownish purple in winter.

Siberian cypress perform best in full sun and well-drained, reasonably fertile soil. However, it is the most shade-tolerant coniferous ground cover, making it more versatile than similar-looking junipers. It is bothered by few pests or diseases. Propagation is by fall cuttings. Hardy to zone 3, it may be grown throughout Atlantic Canada.

Microbiota decussata.
LEFT: *Larix decidua* 'Pendula'.

Picea mariana 'Nana'.

Picea
SPRUCE

Numerous spruce species are grown in Atlantic Canada, with many dwarf forms. The region has three native species. *Picea rubens*, red spruce, is rarely seen in the landscape trade. Black spruce, *P. mariana*, has a cultivar called 'Nana', which forms an irregular blue-green mound up to 60 centimetres tall. White spruce, *P. glauca*, has many named dwarf selections; the most popular, 'Conica', commonly called dwarf Alberta spruce, forms a bright green, tight pyramid 4 metres tall. Rainbow's End™ is similar but the new growth is yellow, turning green as it matures. 'Jean's Dilly', a blue-tinted, smaller version of Alberta spruce, reaches 1.7 metres tall. With a broader pyramidal form is the 1.5-metre-tall, dark green 'Cy's Wonder'. Among the dwarf globular forms of white spruce are bright green 'Alberta Globe' and blue-tinted 'Echinoformis', and, less than 30 centimetres tall, the bright green-coloured 'Little Globe'.

The most popular western North American spruce grown as a garden ornamental is blue spruce, *P. pungens*. Two of the more popular globular forms are 'Glauca Globosa' and 'Mont-

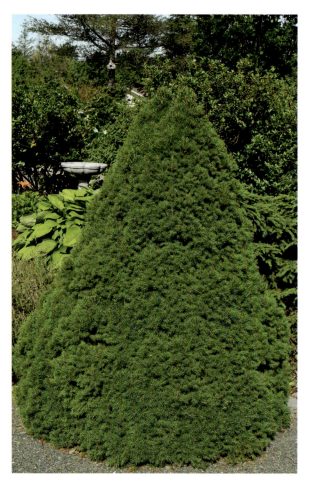

Picea glauca 'Conica'.

gomery', the latter becoming broadly pyramidal with age. Both are generally less than 2 metres tall with steel blue foliage. At 2 to 3 metres tall and with a broad pyramidal habit are 'Corbet' and 'Thume'. With a nestlike form is 'St. Mary's Broom'. Perhaps the more unusual blue spruce is 'Dietz Prostrate', whose stems trail along the ground; it is essentially grown as a ground cover. From western North America also is Sitka spruce, *P. sitchensis*. Two noteworthy dwarf globular forms less than 2 metres tall are 'Christine Berkaw' and 'Papoose', both with sharp-pointed, stiff, blue-tinted needles.

Of the Eurasian species of spruce, the most popular is Norway spruce, *P. abies*. Many dwarf forms of this tree have been selected over the

Picea abies 'Clanbrassiliana'.

years. Among the smallest of the narrow pyramidal forms is 'Pyramidata', which can slowly reach 3 metres. Those with broadly pyramidal growth which reaches 1.5 metres tall include 'Clanbrassiliana', 'Hystrix', and 'Mucronata'. 'Nidiformis', the classic nest spruce, forms a flat-topped globe mostly less than 1 metre tall. A few suggested globular to mounding cultivars that remain less than 60 centimetres are 'Eva', 'Little Gem', 'Pumila', 'Pygmaea', and 'Thumbelina'. 'Pendula' is a top grated weeping form usually grafted at 1 to 1.5 metres, with branches that sweep to the ground then become prostrate, creating a unique skirtlike effect. For a strong contrast, try 'Acro-Yellow', which has brilliant yellow new growth on a dwarf pyramidal plant reaching 3 to 4 metres tall. Serbian spruce, *P. omorika*, has a dwarf pyramidal selection called 'Nana', which can reach 3 metres. 'Pimoko' and 'Kamenz' form rounded, blue-tinted mounds up to 30 centimetres tall. Oriental spruce, *P. orientalis*, has two popular selections that have a low, mounding habit: 'Bergman's Gem' and 'Tom Thumb'. The former is dark green, the latter golden yellow.

The above dwarf spruce cultivars are popular in rock garden settings or bonsai. Some lend themselves to containers, foundations, patio perimeters, or as lawn specimens. All spruce perform best in full sun and acidic, organic-rich, well-drained soil. With the exception of black spruce, all spruce mentioned have some tolerance to drought, except black spruce. Black spruce, however, tolerates wet soil. Spruce budworm is the most common pest, while needle cast and rust are the main diseases. Propagation is by fall cuttings or grafting. The hardiest of the above spruce is black, at zone 2, and blue, at zone 3. Norway, Serbian, and white spruce are hardy to zone 4, while Sitka and Oriental are rated to zone 5.

Picea pungens 'St. Mary's Broom'.

Pinus mugo var. *pumilio*.

Pinus
PINE

There are about 125 species of pines, all native to the northern hemisphere. A few are small enough to be included as shrubs. The most obvious is mugo pine, *Pinus mugo*. The straight species is a large shrub reaching 6 metres tall, but most of the cultivars on the market are significantly shorter, rarely over 2 metres, and, with proper pruning, can be maintained at less than 1 metre. The variety *pumilio* is common in the trade; it forms a large mound up to 1.5 metres tall. Other popular cultivars are 'Mops' (2 metres), 'Sherwood Compact' (1 metre), 'Frisby' (1 metre), 'Bonnie Jean' (30 centimetres), 'Valley Cushion' (30 centimetres), and 'Jakobsen' (30 centimetres). Eastern white pine, *P. strobus*, is native to Atlantic Canada. Several dwarf forms with characteristic soft, blue-green needles are available. 'Blue Shag' has steel blue foliage and forms a tight mound up to 2 metres tall. 'Nana Compacta' is similar. Among the smallest are

Pinus mugo 'Sherwood Compact'.

Pinus strobus 'Nana'.

Pseudotsuga menziesii 'Fletcheri'.

'Sea Urchin' and 'Minuta', both of which form a rounded mound up to 60 centimetres tall. Japanese white pine, *P. parviflora*, is similar to eastern white pine. A popular dwarf selection is 'Adcock's Dwarf', which has an irregular habit up to 1.5 metres tall. 'Catherine Elizabeth' mounds to 1 metre. Among Scots pine, *P. sylvestris*, the most popular dwarf is 'Hillside Creeper', with sprawling stems to 60 centimetres tall but 3 metres wide. 'Albyn Prostrate' is similar in size but has distinctly blue-tinted needles. Among the smallest are 'Janssen Witch', 'Kelpie', and 'Little Ann'. 'Glauca Nana' and 'Beuvronensis' have a rounded habit and may look like they will stay small, but, with time, can eventually reach 3 metres. *P. densiflora* 'Low Glow' forms a dense low mound up to 1.2 metres tall.

Dwarf pines need full sun and regular, well-drained soil. They tolerate some drought but not poorly drained soil. Watch for pine rust on *P. strobus* and *P. parviflora*. The only serious pest is pine sawfly. Propagation is by fall cuttings or grafting. Hardiness varies: zone 3 for *P. mugo* and *P. strobus*; zone 4, *P. sylvestris*; and zone 5, *P. parviflora* and *P. densiflora*.

Pseudotsuga menziesii
DOUGLAS-FIR

Douglas-fir, *Pseudotsuga menziesii*, is native to western North America, where it grows over 25 metres tall. Most of the few dwarfs on the market have mounding or globular habits, reaching 1 to 1.5 metres: 'Loggerhead', 'Densa', 'Fletcheri', and 'Globosa'. The smallest cultivars, at only 30 centimetres tall, are 'Idaho Gem' and 'Hillside Pride'. Two recommended dwarf pyramidal selections are 'Nana' and 'Pygmaea'. Any of the above are suitable for rock gardens, containers, or bonsai.

Douglas-fir prefer full sun and organic, evenly moist soil. It does not tolerate drought. Pests and diseases are rare. Propagation of the dwarf forms is by fall cuttings or grafting. While the regular species is hardy to zone 4, the tenderer dwarf selections are rated for zone 5.

Taxus
YEW

Two main species of yew are grown in Atlantic Canada in addition to their hybrid: English yew, *Taxus baccata*; Japanese yew, *T. cuspidata*; and Anglojap yew, *T.* X *media*. While the species can reach treelike sizes, the majority of the culti-

Taxus cuspidata 'Aurescens'.

Taxus baccata 'Silver Spire'.

vars offered in the nursery trade are essentially shrubs. Even the taller forms are often clipped to less than 2 metres. All yew have flattened dark green needles. Plants are dioecious, with separate male and female plants. Rather than cones, females produce a red cup-shaped fruit with an exposed central seed.

Most cultivars of English yew are 2 to 4 metres tall, with a stiffly upright habit. They add architectural elements to the landscape. As they do not take up much horizontal space, they may be used in smaller gardens. 'Fastigiata Aurea' and 'Silver Spire' are particularly striking, with their yellow-edged needles. For rockeries, try the 45-centimetre-tall 'Green Diamond', a tight congested form with small needles. Japanese yew generally has a more wide-spreading habit. For contrast in the garden, consider 'Aurescens', with yellow-edged needles; 'Bright Gold', whose new growth is bright yellow; and 'Silver Queen', whose new growth has frosty white tips. These

Taxus X *media* 'Hicksii'.

are all mostly less than 1.5 metres tall. 'Minute Westons' has a tight columnar form and can reach 2 metres. 'Capitata' is the popular pyramidal yew. Although it is naturally pyramidal in shape, it does need regular pruning to keep it tight; it reaches 2 to 4 metres tall.

By far the most popular are the Anglojap yews, which are often clipped into globes, boxes, or hedges. With a naturally rounded habit are 'Densiformis', 'Brownii', and 'Fairview'; more upright habit, 'Hicksii' and 'Hillii'; a very narrow columnar form, 'Maureen' and 'H. M. Eddie'. Those with a low spreading habit include 'Dark Green Spreader', 'Tauntonii', and 'Wardii'. Anglojap yew also has a spreading golden form, 'Sunburst'.

Yew tolerate full sun to full shade but those with yellow foliage do not develop their proper coloration without at least partial sun. The narrow columnar forms perform better with full sun. They prefer fertile, well-drained soil and tolerate some drought once they are established. They are poor candidates for wet or salty sites. Exposure to cold winter winds can significantly burn the foliage. Yews are very adaptable to pruning and can bounce back from severe pruning, unlike other needled evergreens. For the most part, they are not bothered by pests or diseases. Yews are highly toxic, except for the red pulp on the female fruit, which is edible. Propagation is by summer or fall cuttings. Japanese and Anglojap yew are hardy to zone 5; English yew, rated for zone 6, is suitable only for the mildest areas of Atlantic Canada.

Thuja occidentalis 'Woodwardii'.

Thuja occidentalis
Eastern white cedar

Eastern white cedar, *Thuja occidentalis*, is native throughout east-central North America, especially around the Great Lakes. The Latin name *Thuja* means tree of life, a reference to the medicinal qualities of the plant. It can form a 15-metre tree. It has become one of the more popular landscape evergreens selected for either its tight pyramidal habit or globular forms. The popular 'Emerald' and 'Holmstrup' are a little tall to be included with shrubs. Pyramidal selections which generally grow to 3 to 4 metres include 'Boisbriand', 'Brobecks Tower', and 'Techny'. The best smaller pyramidal forms with golden foliage are 'Yellow Ribbon' and 'Europe Gold'. Quite different is 'Sherwood Frost', a conical form with cream-tipped new growth.

The most common dwarf cedars are those with a globular form. The classic globe cedar, 'Woodwardii', can reach over 2 metres tall. 'Little Giant' is similar but more compact. Even

Thuja occidentalis 'Emerald'.

smaller are 'Tom Thumb', Mr. Bowling Ball™, and 'Teddy', the latter only 50 centimetres tall. The largest of the popular yellow-foliaged globe cedar is 'Golden Globe', which can reach 2 metres. Becoming progressively smaller are 'Golden Champion', 'Golden Tuffet', and 'Harvest Moon', the last around 60 centimetres tall. Of particular note is 'Rheingold', a cultivar with soft growth, globular to mounding habit while young but over time becomes more conical. It can reach 1.5 metres tall. The new growth is

Thuja occidentalis 'Rheingold'.

coppery gold turning bright yellow but taking on bronzy orange tints in the winter.

The upright pyramidal forms of white cedar are popular for foundation plantings and patio borders, or may be used for hedging, with 'Boisbriand' particularly well suited to this purpose. The globular forms are also popular foundation plants or commonly grown along the edges of driveways or patios. With their distinct growth forms, cedar are classic plants for formal garden settings.

White cedar perform best in full sun but tolerates part shade. Ideally, the soil should be evenly moist and alkaline; in much of Atlantic Canada, a yearly dusting of lime is beneficial. It does not tolerate drought or salt. Insect pests are not common, but deer and moose may browse it. The most serious disease is tip blight. Heavy snow load can damage white cedar and severe winter burn can occur if it is grown in a cold windy site. Propagation is by fall cuttings. It is hardy to zone 3.

Thujopsis dolobrata
HIBA ARBORVITAE

This uncommon conifer is endemic to Japan, where it can reach 25 metres tall. *Thujopsis dolobrata* is the only species in the genus. Its flat fanlike arrangement of scalelike needles looks superficially like eastern white ceder, *Thuja occidentalis*. However, *Thujopsis dolobrata* has larger needles, with distinctive white undersides. The only dwarf is 'Nana'. This plant has a dense, flat-topped, rounded form reaching 60 to 90 centimetres tall. The foliage is naturally yellowish green. It is useful in rock gardens or containers.

Hiba arborvitae prefer full sun to part shade and average, evenly moist well-drained soil that is slightly alkaline. In most parts of Atlantic Canada, a yearly dusting with lime is beneficial. It does not tolerate drought. Pest and diseases are rare. Propagation is by fall cuttings. Hiba arborvitae is rated for zone 5.

Thujopsis dolobrata 'Nana'.

Tsuga canadensis
EASTERN HEMLOCK

Hemlock are generally tall, small-needled trees, native to North America or Asia. Among dwarf types suitable for Atlantic Canada are various selections of native eastern hemlock, *Tsuga canadensis*. Over 50 selections less than 2 metres tall exist, but many are rare and available only from specialist nurseries. Most of the dwarfs have globular or mounding forms. Some of the more common include 'Abbot's Pygmy' (aka 'Pygmaea'), 'Jeddeloh', 'Nana', 'Globosa', 'Little Joe', and 'Horstmann'. With very tight, broadly pyramidal habit are 'Jervis' and 'Jacqueline Verkade'. Low mounding with arching, pendant branches is 'Pendula'; it has spectacular

Tsuga canadensis 'Jeddeloh'.

Tsuga canadensis 'Nana'.

Tsuga canadensis 'Pendula'.

architectural form. 'Cole's Prostrate', a selection only 15 centimetres tall, forms a trailing mat of foliage. All are ideal subjects for rock gardens, alpine troughs, or bonsai.

Hemlock require full sun to part shade and evenly moist, organic-rich slightly acidic soil. It does not tolerate droughty conditions. It is one of the most shade-tolerant conifers, next to yews. Pests and diseases are not common. Propagation is by fall cuttings. While eastern hemlock is hardy to zone 3, many of the dwarf selections are tenderer and suggested for zone 4.

VINES

Actinidia kolomicta.
PREVIOUS SPREAD: *Clematis* 'Romantika'.

Actinidia
KIWI

All of the *Actinidia* species are native to Asia. The hardy kiwi, *A. arguta*, may be grown for both its grape-sized edible fruit and its ability to rapidly twine, up to 8 metres, over pergolas, trellises, and arbours. The waxy foliage is ovate in outline, deep green in summer and turning bright yellow in autumn. Two-centimetre-diameter white flowers are produced in clusters in June or July. Plants are dioecious, with separate male and females; both are needed to produce fruit. 'Dumbarton Oaks' is a popular male; 'Meader', a popular female. If you can find it, try 'Issai', which has perfect flowers and, therefore, fruit with only one plant. It is also smaller, up to 6 metres tall.

Grown for its decorative foliage, but also with edible fruit, is variegated kiwi vine, *A. kolomikta*. It too is a vigorous twining vine which reaches 6 metres. Its heart-shaped leaves are larger than those of *A. arguta*, up to 12 centimetres long, and its leaves appear to have been dipped in white or pink paint. Some leaves are almost entirely pink or white; others have colour only at the extreme tips. Males plants are generally more variegated than the females.

Hardy kiwi grow best in full sun and any reasonably well-drained soil. While part shade is tolerated, the summer and fall foliage colour is less intense and fruit production is limited. Kiwi have few insect or diseases problems. Propagation is by summer cuttings. Both are hardy to zone 4.

Akebia quinata
CHOCOLATE VINE

Native to Japan and China, *Akebia quinata*, also known as fiveleaf akebia or chocolate vine, is not a commonly grown plant in Atlantic Canada but is surprisingly hardy and a fast-growing twining vine which can reach 14 metres if given enough support. It has 3- to 8-centimetre-diameter pal-

Akebia quinata.

mately compound leaves with five elliptical leaflets. The leaf upper surfaces are bright green; undersides are waxy and pale. It has no appreciable fall colour. In June, plants produce hanging clusters of small but fragrant chocolate-purple flowers. Flowers are monoecious, with separate male and female flowers in each cluster. Female flowers will develop sausagelike fruit up to 10 centimetres long. The pulp inside the fruit is edible, adding to the interest of this plant.

Chocolate vine grow in sun to part shade but tolerate more shade than most flowering vines. The soil should be well drained and reasonably fertile. This care-free plant has few pest or disease problems. Do not plant near other trees or shrubs, as it can strangle its timid neighbours. Propagation is by summer cuttings. It is hardy to zone 4.

Ampeliopsis glandulosa ssp. *brevipedunculata*
Porcelain vine

The genus name *Ampeliopsis* comes from the Greek *ampelos*, a grape vine, and *opsis*, likeness, referring to the similarity between porcelain vine and grapes. A single species, *A. glandulosa* ssp. *brevipedunculata*, is grown in Atlantic Canada. This Asian species can reach 6 metres tall. Plants climb by tendrils. Their lightly glossy leaves are palmately lobed and appear similar to those of grapes. They turn bright yellow in autumn. Insignificant tiny green axillary flower clusters develop into attractive fruit that change from pink to lilac to blue as they mature. They are best used on arbours or pergolas. If plants get out of control, hard-prune them close to the ground. As they flower on new wood, they produce some fruit even after such drastic pruning. 'Elegans', a popular selection with white marbled foliage, is invasive south of the border but does not seem to have this tendency in Atlantic Canada.

Porcelain vine grow best in full sun and any well-drained soil. It is shade-tolerant but produces little fruit. Diseases are rare, and the only troublesome insect is Japanese beetle. Propagation is by summer cuttings. It is hardy to zone 4.

Ampeliopsis glandulosa ssp. *brevipedunculata.*

Aristolochia macrophylla.

Aristolochia macrophylla
Dutchman's pipe

This vine, native to the eastern US, is uncommon in Atlantic Canada. Its main claim to fame is its huge 20-centimetre-diameter heart-shaped leaves, which impart a tropical effect to the landscape. A fast-growing twining vine, it can reach 10 metres in height. In June and July, it produces unusual 5-centimetre-long pipe-shaped greenish brown flowers, generally hidden under the leaves. The fall colour is yellow. The species is also sold in the nursery trade as *Aristolochia durior*.

Aristolochia macrophylla.

Dutchman's pipe grow in sun or part shade and any evenly moist soil. It is not drought-tolerant. As it prefers alkaline soil, in most of Atlantic Canada a yearly dusting of lime is beneficial. Pests and diseases are uncommon. Propagation is by summer cuttings or seed. It is rated hardy to zone 4.

Campsis radicans
Trumpet creeper

Trumpet creeper, *Campsis radicans*, is native to the southeast US. This vine, which can reach 12 metres, clings to wood and brickwork by specialized aerial rootlets, similar to English ivy. Its leaves are shiny green, pinnately compound, and up to 40 centimetres long. The fall colour is yellow.

Campsis radicans.

Clusters of 8-centimetre-long, orange-red, trumpet-shaped flowers are produced in midsummer and into fall. 'Flamenco' has orange flowers with red throats, while 'Flava' has yellow flowers. *Campsis* X *tagliabuana*, sometimes seen, is a hybrid between American trumpet creeper and Chinese trumpet creeper, *C. grandiflora*, which reaches 5 metres length. 'Indian Summer', aka 'Kudian', has light orange flowers with a red throat, while 'Madame Galen' has salmon red flowers. Trumpet creeper flowers are relished by hummingbirds and bumblebees. This vine can spread rapidly via seeds or suckers. However, it can be hard-pruned to keep it restrained. As it blooms on new wood, such pruning will not prevent flowering.

Trumpet creeper need full sun, average soil, and, in particular, a warm location in Atlantic Canada. For that reason, it performs best in warm inland locations of Nova Scotia. It is not bothered by pests or diseases. Propagation is by seed, summer cuttings, or sucker removal. It is hardy to zone 5, with the caveat that it needs a warm location to thrive.

Celastrus orbiculatus.

Celastrus
BITTERSWEET

Two species of bittersweet vine are grown in Atlantic Canada: Oriental bittersweet, *Celastrus orbiculatus*, and American bittersweet, *C. scandens*. Both are fast-growing, suckering, deciduous, twining vines that may reach 10 metres in length. They have elliptical to almost circular leaves that turn bright yellow in autumn. Plants are dioecious, with inconspicuous yellow-green male or female flowers produced on separate plants in June. Oriental bittersweet flowers are axillary, while those of American bittersweet are terminal. Female flowers become small globular yellow fruit that split to reveal bright orange-red seeds that, if not eaten by birds, often remain decorative through much of the winter. The most popular heavy-fruiting female clone of *C. scandens* is 'Diana'. However, if you have room for only one plant, try Autumn Revolution®, which has male and female flowers on the same plant.

Bittersweet grow in sun or part shade in any well-drained soil. It is drought-tolerant once established. Do not plant it to climb trees or shrubs, as it can strangle its host. Oriental bittersweet is considered an invasive species in many parts of the US. Few pests or diseases bother it. Propagation is by seed or summer or hardwood cuttings. Both are hardy to zone 3.

Clematis alpina 'Willy'.

LEFT: *Clematis* 'Bees Jubilee'.

Clematis
Clematis

Clematis is the queen of flowering vines. The over 300 species of clematis have worldwide distribution. Some are herbaceous perennials, while most are vines, both deciduous and evergreen. In regards to those hardy vines grown in Atlantic Canada, only deciduous species and hybrids are grown. They fall into three main groups, based on their pruning requirements. Group 1 flower on old wood and generally do not require any significant pruning other than trimming to keep them in bounds. Group 2 flower on both new and old wood. They often produce a large flush of flowers in early summer to midsummer, followed by occasional flowers later in the season, or they may bloom continuously all season.

They may be hard-pruned if needed but generally only need light pruning to remove the dead stems and to keep them within bounds. Group 3 flower only on new wood. They are hard-pruned close to the ground every spring. They flower in late summer or early autumn. Climbing clematis attach themselves to shrubs, trees, trellises, arbours, and pergolas by twisting their leaf petioles around the supporting structure.

Group 1 clematis have species that bloom in spring, summer, or fall. Among the spring bloomers are *C. alpina* and *C. macropetala*. Both have 3- to 6-centimetre-diameter nodding flowers with four tepals, blooming in May and June. They generally reach 2.5 to 3 metres tall. Popular cultivars of *C. alpina* include 'Blue Dancer' (light blue), 'Constance' (deep pink), 'Pame-

Clematis alpina 'Pamela Jackman'.

la Jackman' (deep blue), 'Ruby' (reddish pink), and 'Willy' (light pink). Among *C. macropetala* is 'Jan Lindmark' (mauve purple), 'Lagoon' (blue), 'Maidwell Hall' (blue), 'Purple Spider' (reddish purple), and 'White Swan'. The borderline hardy *C. montana* is also a spring bloomer. These have open flowers, about 5 to 7 centimetres wide, with four rounded tepals. 'Rubens' has pink flowers, while 'Grandiflora' has white. Blooming midsummer with nodding, bell-like flowers is *C. tangutica* (yellow) and *C. orientalis* (yellow). Midsummer hybrids of this group include 'My Angel' (purple reverse, yellow inside), 'Bill Mackenzie' (golden yellow), and 'Radar Love' (yellow with purple stamens). The fall-blooming Group 1 clematis have sprays of small white, oftentimes fragrant, flowers. These include Virgin's bower, *C. virginiana*, and the closely related *C. paniculata* var. *ternifolia*. All of the above produce attractive fluffy seed heads that often remain on the plant well into the fall.

The Group 2 clematis are the standard clematis, with dinner-plate-shaped flowers up to 15 centimetres or more wide. Hundreds of hybrids are available, with colours ranging from white through shades of pink, red, purple, and blue, with the addition of bicolours. Popular hybrids include 'Bees Jubilee' (two-tone pink), 'Blue Ravine' (light blue), 'Carnaby' (two-tone pink), 'Daniel Deronda' (blue), 'Elsa Spath' (lavender blue), 'Ernest Markham' (red), 'Henryi' (white), 'Madame le Coultre' (white), 'Nelly Moser' (two-tone pink), 'Pink Chiffon' (light pink), 'President' (purple), 'Ramona' (lavender-blue), 'Rouge Cardinal' (red), and 'Westerplatte' (red). Double-flowered hybrids include 'Innocent Glance' (pink), 'Multi Blue' (blue), and 'Proteus' (mauve-pink).

The more popular Group 3 clematis are selections of *C. vitacella*. These have 5- to 8-centimetre-diameter flowers in late summer-early autumn. Popular cultivars include 'Dark Eyes' (deep purple), 'Etoile Violette' (purple), 'Madame Julia Correvon' (red), 'Minuet' (creamy white), 'Polish Spirit' (reddish purple), and 'Venosa' (dark purple). Perhaps the most famous of the Group 3 clematis is 'Jackmanii', with dark velvet purple flowers. Other popular larger-flowered clematis from this group are 'Blue Angel' (lavender-blue), 'Caroline' (light pink), 'Marga-

Clematis tangutica.

Clematis 'Ville de Lyon'.

Hedera helix
ENGLISH IVY

Popular as a houseplant, English ivy may also be grown outdoors in milder areas of Atlantic Canada. The toughest of the English ivies is *Hedera helix* var. *baltica*. It has palmate, leathery, deep green leaves with three to five lobes. In winter, the leaves may take on a dark purple tint. This variety grows much faster than the typical houseplant English ivy. Self-clinging by aerial roots, it sticks to any rough surface such as brickwork, wood, and rough-barked trees. It reaches 20 metres or more if grown vertically or may be grown as a broad-leaved evergreen ground cover, where it reaches 15 to 20 centimetres tall. English ivy has both a juvenile and adult form. The juvenile is the classic clinging vine; the adult develops at the top of vertical-growing plants. This form has rounded leaves, twiggy, non-climbing stems, and develops umbels of green flowers in early autumn, which develop into black fruit that remain through the winter.

ret Hunt' (lilac pink), 'Romantica' (deep purple), 'Star of India' (reddish purple), 'Skyfall' (pale blue), and 'Ville de Lyon' (reddish pink). The *C. texensis* cultivars have 5- to 8-centimetre-diameter tulip-shaped flowers. Popular selections include 'Duchess of Albany' (medium pink), 'Gravetye Beauty' (red), 'Princess Diana' (deep pink), 'Princess Kate' (white with purple-pink reverse), and 'Radiance' (pale violet blue).

Clematis, as a group, need full sun and evenly moist but well-drained, slightly acidic, fertile soil. However, they grow better if their roots are shaded. None tolerate droughty conditions. Insect pests are uncommon, but diseases include powdery mildew and a fatal disease called clematis wilt. Planting them up to 15 centimetres deeper than they were growing in their purchased state can reduce the incidence of wilt. Propagation is by summer cuttings or, in the case of species, seed. Hardiness varies, with *C. alpina*, *C. macropetala*, and *C. tangutica* the hardiest, suitable for zone 3. Most of the standard clematis as well as Virgin's bower are rated for zone 4. *Clematis texensis*, *C. vitacella*, and *C. paniculata* var. *ternifolia* are rated for zone 5. *Clematis montana* is the most tender, suitable only for the warmest areas of zone 6 in southern Nova Scotia.

Hedera helix.

Hedera helix 'Gold Heart'.

Many of the houseplant selections of English ivy are not as hardy as the variety *baltica*. Some smaller-leaved, slower-growing selections worth trying in the mildest areas are 'Needlepoint', green leaves reminiscent of bird's feet; 'Glacier', grey-green leaves with irregular white margins; and 'Gold Child', yellow-edged leaves. Particularly striking is 'Gold Heart', whose deep green leaves have a large central yellow blotch.

English ivy grow in part to full shade. Full sun, particularly in winter, can scorch the leaves. It performs best with fertile soil. Few pests or diseases bother it. Propagation is by summer cuttings. The variety *baltica* is hardy to zone 5, while the others are more reliable in zone 6.

Humulus lupulus
Hops

Hops was originally grown for the female seed pods, which are the main flavouring for beer. However, hops can be grown for its ornamental value as well. Hops, an herbaceous vine that arises from a thickened, woody rootstock, can reach to 15 metres in a single season. Hops climbs by twining around any substrate it comes into contact with. Plants are dioecious, with separate male and female plants, but the flowers of both sexes are insignificant. The leaves are palmate with three to five lobes and have coarsely serrated margins. The mix of yellow and brown fall colour is not particularly striking. The main ornamental selection is 'Aureus', whose leaves are golden yellow all season if grown in full sun, but chartreuse if grown in less than full sun. A fast-growing vine, it is particularly suited to growing over pergolas, arbours, and similar structures but it can also grow up tree trunks. As the stems are deciduous, it is best to cut it back to the ground each fall or early spring.

Hops need full sun to part shade and perform best with fertile, evenly moist soil, but tolerate some drought, once established. It is a care-free plant, with no serious pests or diseases. Propagation is by basal cuttings in spring. It is hardy to zone 3.

Hydrangea anomala ssp. *petiolaris*.

Hydrangea anomala ssp. *petiolaris*
Climbing hydrangea

Climbing hydrangea, *H. anomala* ssp. *petiolaris*, is a climbing deciduous vine which clings to trees, brickwork, wood, and similar substrates via adventitious roots. This East Asian species can potentially reach 16 metres but is often less than 10 metres. It has rounded to heart-shaped leaves which turn brilliant yellow in autumn. Its fragrant, white, flat-topped clusters of flowers are produced in June and July. Like most hydrangea, the flower clusters are a mix of small fertile flowers and larger sterile flowers. 'Miranda' is an outstanding variegated selection whose leaves have yellow margins.

Humulus lupulus 'Aureus'.

Hydrangea anomala ssp. *petiolaris*.

Climbing hydrangea grow in full sun to considerable shade. It is perhaps the best flowering vine to grow on a north-facing wall. The soil should be fertile and evenly moist. This care-free climber has few pests or diseases. Propagation is by summer cuttings. It is hardy to zone 4.

Lonicera
HONEYSUCKLE

The many species and hybrids of twining honeysuckle may quickly reach 6 metres or more, making them ideal for arbours, trellises, pergolas, and fences. The genus name honors German botanist Adam Lonitzer (1528–1586). An heirloom or heritage species in Atlantic Canada is common honeysuckle or European woodbine, *Lonicera periclymenum*. This species has waxy, deep green leaves that are pale blue-green below. The two-lipped, tubular, highly fragrant flowers are produced in a terminal whorl from July to frost. Petals are white inside and pink on the outside, but turn golden yellow as they age. These later develop into glossy red fruit. 'Serotina' and 'Belgica' are earlier cultivars, the former has broader and shorter floral tubes than the latter. Other recent cultivars include 'Heaven Scent' and 'Scentsation', both with white flowers that age to pale yellow. Also highly scented, with white

Hydrangea petiolaris 'Miranda'.

Lonicera 'Gold Flame'.
RIGHT: *Lonicera* 'Mandarin'.

190   SHRUBS AND VINES FOR ATLANTIC CANADA

to pale yellow flowers, is Japanese honeysuckle, *L. japonica*. This species is vigorous and could potentially become invasive. 'Halliana' is the standard cultivar. A newer hybrid is *L.* X *heckrottii* 'Gold Flame', which has two-tone deep pink and golden flowers. If variegated foliage is your preference, try *L.* X *italica* Harlequin™, whose leaves are edged in white.

Another group of twining honeysuckle have trumpet-shaped flowers in shades of yellow, orange, and red but unfortunately lack any strong fragrance. These include *L. sempervirens* 'Major Wheeler' (reddish orange), *L. sempervirens* 'John Clayton' (bright yellow), *L. sempervirens* 'Blance Sandman' (pinkish red), and the hybrids *L.* X *brownii* 'Dropmore Scarlet' (deep orange-red), *L.* X *brownii* Honeybelle™ (bright yellow), and *L.* 'Mandarin' (bright orange). While all twining honeysuckle are attractive to butterflies, hawkmoths, and hummingbirds, this second group is a hummingbird magnet.

These honeysuckles bloom best if grown in full sun with organic-rich, evenly moist soil. The most common disease is powdery mildew. The main insect pests are small moth larvae, which can be particularly damaging to flower buds. Leafroller moths may also be problematic. Propagation is by summer or hardwood cuttings. All the above are hardy to zone 4.

Lonicera periclymenum 'Belgica'.

Lonicera X *brownii* 'Dropmore Scarlet'.

Parthenocissus tricuspidata.

Parthenocissus
Virginia creeper, Boston ivy

The 12 species of *Parthenocissus* are native to Asia or North America. The genus name is Greek and translates "virgin ivy." Two species are grown in Atlantic Canada: Virginia creeper, *P. quinquefolia*, and Boston ivy, *P. tricuspidata*. Virginia creeper, native to eastern North America, is a fast-growing climber that attaches itself by specialized tendrils that end in suction-cup-like appendages. Its leaves are relatively large, palmately compound with five serrated, glossy elliptical leaflets. Its main claim to fame is its spectacular scarlet fall foliage. Rather insignificant yellow-green flowers become small clusters of blue fruit. Virginia creeper clings to any rough surface and can be destructive on wooden or vinyl siding; grow on brick or stonework instead. It also climbs into the upper canopy of trees. 'Engelmannii' is the main cultivar sold, but worth looking for is Star Showers®, which has leaves prettily mottled in white or pink. 'Yellow Wall' is a selection whose fall colour is yellow rather than red.

Parthenocissus quinquefolia.

Boston ivy, despite the name, is native to China and Japan. However, the common name refers to the fact that it is often grown on the stone and brick buildings of eastern US colleges and universities. It is slower growing than Virginia creeper, but, like Virginia creeper, it can reach 15 metres tall in time. Its leaves are trilobed and develop beautiful scarlet to burgundy fall foliage. Its insignificant flowers develop into clusters of small blue fruit. A popular cultivar is 'Veitchii', whose spring leaves are purple-tinted and smaller than those of the regular Boston ivy.

Both of these ivies may be grown in sun or shade but the best fall colour results from full sun. Any well-drained soil will suffice. Both are quite drought-tolerant. Pests and diseases are rare. Propagation is by summer or hardwood cuttings. Virginia creeper is hardy to zone 3; Boston ivy, rated for zone 4.

Polygonum aubertii
Silver lace vine

Silver lace vine is known in the nursery trade as *Polygonum aubertii*, but its correct botanical name is *Fallopia baldschuanica*. This twining vine, native to western China and Tibet, reaches a height of 8 metres. Its unique arrowhead-shaped leaves, up to 10 centimetres long, are bright green in summer, turning yellow in autumn. From midsummer to frost, it produces frothy sprays of tiny, white, fragrant flowers. It is a vigorous vine suitable for arbours and pergolas—but keep it away from neighbouring trees and shrubs, as it can swamp them.

Silver lace vine grow in any type of soil as long as it is well drained. Full sun provides the best floral display. Diseases are not a problem, but Japanese beetles and leaf miners can occasionally attack it. Propagation is by summer cuttings. It is hardy to zone 4.

Polygonum aubertii.

Rosa 'John Cabot'.

Rosa
Rambling/climbing Rose

Botanically, rambling and climbing roses are shrubs with long flexible stems, not true vines or climbers. Rambling roses have the most flexible stems, allowing them to be easily trained along arbours, trellises, and pergolas. They may easily reach 3 to 6 metres tall. Their flowers are in clusters of seven or more and they typically have seven leaflets. Most have a single flush of blooms. Climbing roses have much stiffer canes—easy to accommodate on trellises, not so easy over arbours and pergolas. They more commonly have flowers in clusters of five, and each leaf has five leaflets. Many are repeat bloomers.

Three of the oldest ramblers are 'Dorothy Perkins' (pink), 'Excelsa' (aka 'Red Dorothy Perkins'), and 'City of York' (white). All have 3-centimetre-diameter flowers that are only lightly fragrant. 'Albertine' is another hybrid with pale pink flowers up to 8 centimetres wide. 'American Pillar' has very dark green glossy foliage and masses of single, deep reddish pink flowers with white eyes.

Far more climbing roses than ramblers are on the market. Suggested hybrids are 'Blaze' (red),

Rosa 'Albertine'.
LEFT: *Rosa* 'Dorothy Perkins'.

Schizophragma hydrangeoides
Japanese Hydrangea

Closely related to climbing hydrangea, Japanese hydrangea, *Schizophragma hydrangeoides*, is a self-clinging, deciduous plant with sharply serrated, heart-shaped leaves. Like climbing hydrangea, it also turns bright yellow in autumn. It can reach 12 metres in height if given the proper support. Its adventitious roots will stick to any rough surface, especially brick and stonework. Its flowers are much like those of climbing hydrangea—flat-topped clusters of white flowers, which are a mix of small fertile flowers and larger sterile ones. The cultivar 'Moonlight' has silvery green leaves with dark green veins, while Burst of Light® has white-mottled leaves. 'Roseum' has white flowers that age to pink.

'Improved Blaze' (dark red), 'Paul's Scarlet' (red), 'America' (salmon pink), 'Coral Dawn' (coral pink), 'Swan Lake' (pale pink), 'New Dawn' (pale pink), 'Golden Showers' (yellow), and 'White Dawn'. The Explorer roses 'John Cabot' and 'Henry Kelsey' are also considered climbing roses. Many other rambling and climbing roses are available from specialist nurseries.

Roses love sun but the ramblers tolerate part shade and still provide a reasonable floral display. Rich, fertile, well-drained soil provides the best blooms. Roses have their fair share of pests and diseases. Black spot and powdery mildew are the most common diseases; however, several of the above hybrids are resistant. Aphids, leafrollers, and other moth larvae are the main pests. Propagation is by summer cuttings for ramblers or, more often, by grafting for climbers. The ramblers noted above are hardy to zone 4, while the climbers are zones 4 or 5, depending on the hybrid.

Schizophragma hydrangeoides.

Japanese hydrangea grow in full sun to considerable shade and in any fertile, evenly moist soil. Overall, it has a slower rate of growth than climbing hydrangea. It has few pests or diseases. Propagation is by summer cuttings. It is not quite as hardy as climbing hydrangea, being rated for zone 5.

Vitis vinifera
GRAPE

Nearly 80 species of grapes exist, but only a few are grown commercially as eating or wine grapes. Grapes are fast-growing vines that cling by twisting tendrils. They are ideal for growing over pergolas, with the bonus of edible fruit. However, the focus of this book is woody plants grown primarily for their ornamental value. Two grapes are grown solely for their ornamental leaves, both selections of *Vitis vinifera*. The most popular is 'Purpurea', whose summer leaves are tinted purple, but turn blazing scarlet in autumn. 'Variegata' has white-mottled summer leaves that turn golden yellow in autumn. While the fruit of each is edible, it is not particularly tasty. Both can reach 12 metres.

These ornamental grapes need full sun and rich, fertile, well-drained soil. They are carefree, with powdery mildew the only serious disease. Propagation is by summer cuttings. They are hardy to zone 5.

Wisteria
WISTERIA

No climber is as impressive in bloom as a well-grown wisteria. The eight species of wisteria are native to Asia and eastern North America. The genus name honours Caspar Wistar (1761–1818), a professor of anatomy at the University of Pennsylvania. Wisteria are twining vines, up

Wisteria floribunda 'Lawrence'.

to 8 metres tall, with large pinnate leaves similar to those of ash. Shortly before or after they begin to flush leaves, plants produce 15- to 30-centimetre-long, pendant sprays of purple-blue pealike flowers. The foliar fall colour is usually yellow. They are more commonly grown over pergolas and arbours. Traditionally, the Japanese wisteria, *W. floribunda*, was grown. This species needs hard-pruning each fall or winter to keep it in check and encourage flowering. Popular cultivars of Japanese wisteria include 'Macrobotrys', 'Royal Purple', 'Issai', 'Alba', 'Black Dragon', 'Pink Ice', and 'Lawrence', the latter being the hardiest. Silky wisteria, *W. brachybotrys*, is similar but its flower clusters are a little shorter. 'Okayama' has pale lilac flowers, 'Shiro-beni'

Wisteria floribunda 'Black Dragon'.

pale pink, and 'Shiro-kapitan' white. Both Japanese and Silky wisteria have fragrant flowers and start blooming just prior to leafing.

From eastern US is Kentucky wisteria, *W. macrostachya*. It is similar in appearance to the Asian species but it flowers after the leaves have emerged, about two weeks later than the Asian species. It is apt to be a more reliable bloomer but, unfortunately, lacks the wonderful fragrance of the Asian species. However, it is significantly hardier and far less aggressive. 'Blue Moon' is a popular cultivar. Similar and from the southeastern US is also American wisteria, *W. frutescens*, whose flowers, in clusters up to 15 centimetres long, are lightly scented. 'Amethyst Falls' is the most popular cultivar.

Wisteria need full sun and slightly acidic, humus-rich soil. They do not tolerate droughty conditions. Few pests or diseases bother them. Propagation is by summer cuttings. Kentucky wisteria is hardy to zone 4, while American wisteria and the Asian species are rated for zone 5.

PLANT SELECTOR

ONLY PLANTS GENERALLY SELECTED FOR THEIR FLOWERS ARE INCLUDED BELOW.

Latin Name	Common Name	Blooming Season	Light	Height	Page #
Amelanchier	Serviceberry	May–mid-June	Sun to part shade	2–10 m	43
Andromeda polifolia	Bog rosemary	May–June	Sun	10–50 cm	135
Aralia	Devil's walking-stick	August–mid-October	Sun to part shade	3–5 m	44
Arctostaphylos uva-ursi	Bearberry	May–June	Sun to part shade	10 cm	135
Aronia	Chokeberry	June–early July	Sun to part shade	1–4 m	45
Berberis thunbergii	Barberry	May–mid-June	Sun to part shade	1–3 m	46
Buddleja davidii	Butterfly-bush	August–October	Sun	3–5 m	48
Calluna vulgaris	Heather	August–October	Sun	10–60 cm	136
Campsis radicans	Trumpet creeper	August–September	Sun	6–12 m	182
Caragana arborescens	Siberian peashrub	mid-May–June	Sun	1.5–6 m	51
Caryopteris X clandonensis	Bluebeard	August–October	Sun	90 cm	51
Cassiope	Bell heather	May–June	Sun	10–20 cm	137
Cephalanthus occidentalis	Buttonbush	late July–September	Sun to part shade	1–3 m	52
Chaenomeles	Flowering quince	May–mid-June	Sun to part shade	1–3.5 m	53
Clematis	Clematis	May–October	Sun	2.5–3 m	185
Clethra alnifolia	Summersweet	August–October	Sun to part shade	1–2.4 m	56
Cornus sericea	Red-osier dogwood	late May–June	Sun to shade	1–3 m	57
Corylopsis	Winter hazel	mid-April–May	Sun to part shade	2–3 m	58
Cytisus	Broom	June–mid-July	Sun	0.5–2 m	64

SHRUBS AND VINES FOR ATLANTIC CANADA

Daboecia cantabrica	St. Daboec's heath	late June to October	Sun	20-40 cm	138
Daphne	Daphne	April–June	Sun to part shade	0.3-1.5 m	65
Deutzia	Deutzia	June–July	Sun to part shade	0.6-3 m	67
Diervilla lonicera	Bush honeysuckle	June–July	Sun to part shade	1 m	68
Enkianthus campanulatus	Redvein enkianthus	June	Sun to part shade	2-4 m	139
Erica carnea/darleyensis	Spring heath	late March–early June	Sun	10-60 cm	140
Erica tetralix/cinerea/vagans	Summer heath	July to October	Sun	10-60 cm	140
Exocorda X macrantha	Pearlbush	May–June	Sun to part shade	1.2 m	71
Forsythia	Forsythia	mid-April–May	Sun to part shade	1-3 m	71
Fothergilla	Dwarf fothergilla	May–mid-June	Sun to part shade	0.5-3 m	73
Genista	Broom	June–July	Sun	30-90 cm	75
Hamamelis	Witch hazel	late March–early May	Sun to part shade	2-3 m	76
Heptacodium miconioides	Seven-son flower	September–October	Sun	4-5 m	78
Hibiscus syriacus	Rose-of-Sharon	August–October	Sun	2-4 m	78
Hydrangea	Hydrangea	August–October	Sun to part shade	1-8 m	79
Hydrangea anomala ssp. petiolaris	Climbing hydrangea	June–July	Sun to shade	6-10 m	189
Hypericum	St. John's-wort	August–October	Sun	30-90 cm	84
Itea virginica	Sweetspire	mid-June–July	Sun to shade	1-2 m	87
Kerria japonica	Japanese kerria	May–June	Part shade	2-3 m	88
Kalmia latifolia	Mountain laurel	June	Sun to part shade	1.5-2.5 m	143
Kolkwitzia amabilis	Beautybush	June–July	Sun to part shade	2-2.75 m	88
Lavendula angustifolia	English lavender	July–August	Sun	30-45 cm	90
Leiophyllum buxifolium	Sand-myrtle	June	Sun	15-30 cm	145

TODD BOLAND

Latin Name	Common Name	Blooming Season	Light	Height	Page #
Leucothöe fontanesiana	Drooping leucothöe	late May–June	Sun to part shade	1–3 m	146
Lonicera (climbing)	Honeysuckle vine	July to October	Sun to part shade	4–6 m	190
Lonicera tatarica	Tatarian honeysuckle	June	Sun to part shade	2–4 m	91
Magnolia stellata	Star magnolia	late April–May	Sun	3–4 m	92
Mahonia	Grape-holly	May	Part shade to shade	1–2 m	93
Paeonia suffruticosa	Tree peony	mid-June–mid-July	Sun	1–1.5 m	97
Philadelphus	Mock-orange	late June–July	Sun	1–4 m	98
Phyllodoce	Mountain heather	June–early July	Sun	20–30 cm	148
Physocarpus opulifolius	Ninebark	June–mid-July	Sun to part shade	1–3 m	99
Pieris japonica	Japanese andromeda	mid-April–May	Sun to part shade	1–4 m	148
Polygonum aubertii	Silver lace vine	August–September	Sun	4–8 m	194
Potentilla fruticosa	Shrubby cinquefoil	late June–October	Sun	0.5–1.5 m	100
Prunus	Dwarf cherry	May–early June	Sun	2–3 m	102
Pyracantha coccinea	Firethorn	mid-May–mid-June	Sun	2–3 m	103
Rhododendron	Rhododendron/azalea	late April–July	Sun to part shade	0.1–4 m	152
Ribes sanguineum	Flowering currant	May–early June	Sun	2–3 m	105
Rosa	Rose	mid-June–September	Sun	1–4 m	106, 195
Rubus	Flowering raspberry	June–July	Sun to part shade	1–2 m	109
Salix	Pussywillow	March–May	Sun to part shade	1–4 m	110
Sambucus	Elderberry	June–July	Sun to part shade	2–4 m	111
Schizophragma hydrangeoides	Japanese hydrangea	June–July	Sun to shade	6–12 m	197
Sorbaria sorbifolia	Ural false spirea	late June–July	Sun to part shade	2–3 m	115

Spiraea	Spirea	June–July	Sun to part shade	0.5-2.5 m	116
Stephanandra incisa	Lace shrub	June–July	Sun to part shade	60 cm	118
Syringa	Lilac	June–July	Sun	2-6 m	120
Tamarix	Salt-cedar	July–August	Sun	3-5 m	123
Viburnum	Viburnum	June–July	Sun to part shade	1.5-6 m	124
Weigela	Weigela	June–July	Sun to part shade	0.5-3 m	127
Wisteria	Wisteria	late May–early July	Sun	6-8 m	198
X Phylliopsis hillieri	Phylliopsis	June	Sun	15-30 cm	150
Xanthoceras sorbifolium	Yellowhorn	June	Sun	3-7 m	130
Yucca	Yucca	July–August	Sun	2 m	130
Zenobia pulverulenta	Honey-cup	June–July	Sun	1-3 m	157

TODD BOLAND

INDEX
PLANTS BY LATIN NAME

Abies 161
Acer palmatum 42
Actinidia 180
Akebia quinata 180
Amelanchier 43
Ampeliopsis glandulosa
    ssp. *brevipedunculata* 181
Andromeda polifolia 135
Aralia 44
Arctostaphylos uva-ursi 135
Aristolochia macrophylla 182
Aronia 45
Artemisia 46

Berberis 46
Buddleja 48
Buxus 49

Callicarpa dichotoma 50
Calluna vulgaris 136
Campsis radicans 182
Caragana 51
Caryopteris X *clandonensis* 51
Cassiope 137
Celastris 183
Cephalanthus occidentalis 52
Chaenomeles 53
Chamaecyparis 161
Clematis 185
Clethra 56
Cornus 57
Corylopsis 58

Corylus 59
Cotinus coggyria 60
Cotoneaster 62
Cryptomeria 163
Cytisus 64

Daboecia cantabrica 138
Daphne 65
Deutzia 67
Diervilla 68

Eleutherococcus sieboldianus 69
Enkianthus 139
Erica 140
Euonymus 69
Exocorda X *macrantha* 71

Forsythia 71
Fothergilla 73

Gaultheria 142
Genista 75

Hamamelis 76
Hedera helix 187
Heptacodium miconoides 78
Hibiscus syriacus 78
Hippophae rhamnoides 79
Humulus lupulus 188
Hydrangea 79
Hydrangea anomala ssp. *petiolaris* 189
Hypericum 84

Ilex 84
Itea virginica 87

Juniperus 163

Kalmia 143
Kerria japonica 88
Kolkwitzia amabilis 88

Larix 165
Lavendula angustifolia 90
Leiophyllum buxifolium 145
Leucothöe 146
Ligustrum 91
Lonicera (shrub) 91
Lonicera (vine) 190

Magnolia stellata 92
Mahonia 93
Microbiota decussata 167
Morella pensylvanica 94

Pachysandra 95
Pachystima canbyi 95
Paeonia suffruticosa 97
Parthenocissus 193
Pernettya mucronata 147
Philadelphus 98
Phyllodoce 148
Physocarpus opulifolius 99
Picea 168
Pieris 148
Pinus 170
Polygonum aubertii 194
Potentilla fruticosa 100
Prunus 102
Pseudotsuga menziesii 171
Pyracantha coccinea 103

Rhododendron (Rhododendron) 152
Rhododendron (Azalea) 154
Rhus 104
Ribes 105
Rosa (shrub) 106
Rosa (vine) 195
Rubus 109

Salix 110
Sambucus 111
Schizophragma hydrangeoides 197
Skimmia japonica 114
Sorbaria sorbifolia 115
Sorbus 116
Spiraea 116
Stephanandra incisa 118
Symphoricarpos 119
Syringa 120

Tamarix 123
Taxus 171
Thuja occidentalis 174
Thujopsis dolobrata 175
Tsuga canadensis 176

Viburnum 124
Vitis vinifera 198

Weigela 127
Wisteria 198

X *Phylliopsis hillieri* 156
Xanthoceras sorbifolium 130

Yucca 130

Zenobia pulverulenta 157

TODD BOLAND

INDEX

PLANTS BY COMMON NAME

Adam's needle 130
andromeda 148
angelica tree 44
azalea 154

barberry 46
bearberry 135
beautyberry 50
beautybush 88
bittersweet 183
bluebeard 51
bog laurel 143
bog rosemary 135
Boston ivy 193
boxwood 49
boy's-love 46
broom (*Cytisus*) 64
broom (*Genista*) 75
burning bush 69
bush honeysuckle 68
butterfly-bush 48
buttonbush 52

cedar, Japanese 163
chocolate vine 180
chokeberry 45
clematis 185
cliff green 95
climbing hydrangea 189
climbing rose 195
coralberry 119
cotoneaster 62

Daphne 65
deutzia 67
devil's walking-stick 44
dogwood 57
Douglas-fir 171
drooping leucothöe 146
dusty zenobia 157
Dutchman's pipe 182
dwarf fothergilla 73
Dyer's greenwood 75

eastern hemlock 176
eastern white cedar 174
elderberry 111
English ivy 187

false cypress 161
fetterbush 146
fir 161
firethorn 103
five-finger aralia 69
flowering almond 102
flowering currant 105
flowering quince 53
flowering raspberry 109
forsythia 71

grape 198
grape-holly 93

206   SHRUBS AND VINES FOR ATLANTIC CANADA

hazel 59
heath 140
heather 136
hiba arborvitae 175
holly 84
honey-cup 157
honeysuckle (shrub) 91
     bush honeysuckle 68
honeysuckle (vine) 190
hops 188
hydrangea 79
     climbing hydrangea 189
     Japanese hydrangea 197

Japanese cedar 163
Japanese hydrangea 197
Japanese kerria 88
Japanese maple 42
Japanese skimmia 114
juneberry 43
juniper 163

kinnikinnik 135
kiwi 180

lace shrub 118
larch 165
lavender 90
lilac 120

maple, Japanese 42
mock-orange 98
mountain bell heather 137
mountain heather 148
mountain laurel 143
mountain-ash 116

nanking cherry 102
ninebark 99
northern bayberry 94

Oregon-grape 93

pearlbush 71
peashrub 51
pine 170
porcelain vine 181
prickly heath 147
privet 91

rambling rose 195
redvein enkianthus 139
rhododendron 152
rose-of-Sharon 78
roses (shrub) 106
     climbing rose 195
     rambling rose 195

salt-cedar 123
sand-myrtle 145
sea buckthorn 79
serviceberry 43
seven-son flower 78
shadblow 43
shrubby cinquefoil 100
Siberian cypress 167
silver lace vine 194
smokebush 60
smoketree 60
snowberry 119
southernwood 46
spindletree 69
spirea 116
spruce 168
spurge 95
St. Dabeoc's heath 138
St. John's-wort 84
star magnolia 92
sumac 104
summersweet 56
sweet pepperbush 56
sweetspire 87

TODD BOLAND

thimbleberry 109
tree peony 97
trumpetcreeper 182

Ural false spirea 115

viburnum 124
Virginia creeper 193

weigela 127
willow 110

winter hazel 58
wintercreeper 69
wintergreen 142
wisteria 198
witch alder 73
witch-hazel 76

yellowhorn 130
yew 171
yucca 130

ACKNOWLEDGEMENTS

I would like to thank Boulder Books for accepting this book proposal and allowing me to share my love and knowledge of plants and gardening with other Atlantic Canadian gardeners.

Many thanks to Stephanie Porter and Iona Bulgin for their careful attention to the prose of this book. A special thank-you to graphic designer Todd Manning who combined the text and many photos to create this work of beauty.

All photos in this book were taken by author Todd Boland.

Todd Boland is the author of *Favourite Perennials for Atlantic Canada*, *Trees & Shrubs of Newfoundland and Labrador*, *Trees & Shrubs of the Maritimes*, *Wildflowers & Ferns of Newfoundland and Labrador*, *Wildflowers of Nova Scotia*, *Wildflowers of New Brunswick*, and *Wildflowers of Fogo Island and Change Islands*.

Todd has written about and lectured on various aspects of horticulture and native plants internationally. He is a founding member of the Newfoundland and Labrador Wildflower Society and an active website volunteer with the North American Rock Garden Society.

Born and raised in St. John's, Newfoundland and Labrador, Todd graduated from Memorial University of Newfoundland with an M.Sc. in Biology and a specialization in Plant Ecology. Alpine and Asian plants are his longstanding outdoor gardening passion; indoors, he maintains an ever-increasing orchid collection. Photography and bird watching occupy any non-gardening downtime.

NOTES

NOTES

NOTES

NOTES